Praise for *The Leader Phrase Book*

"A truly useful reference book that any white-collar worker should have close to hand."

— Dayne Cowan, Chair of the UK Section of the Visual Effects Society

"Now is your chance to learn the phrases that will make you a success."

— David Kunkler, number-one best-selling video game producer

"A snapshot into how little it takes to quickly master the nuances of language."

—George Bitar, multi-awarded plastic surgeon

The Leader
Phrase Book

*3000+ Powerful Phrases That
Put You in Command*

Patrick Alain

The Career Press, Inc.
Pompton Plains, NJ

THE LEADER PHRASE BOOK
EDITED BY KATE HENCHES
TYPESET BY GINA TALUCCI AND DIANA GHAZZAWI
Printed in the U.S.A.

To order this title, please call toll-free 1-800-CAREER-1 (NJ and Canada: 201-848-0310) to order using VISA or MasterCard, or for further information on books from Career Press.

B CAREER PRESS

The Career Press, Inc.
220 West Parkway, Unit 12
Pompton Plains, NJ 07444
www.careerpress.com

Library of Congress Cataloging-in-Publication Data
Alain, Patrick.
    The leader phrase book : 3,000+ powerful phrases that put you in command / by Patrick Alain.
        p. cm.
    Includes index.
    ISBN 978-1-60163-200-5 -- ISBN 978-1-60163-626-3 (ebook)
1. Business communication. 2. Leadership. 3. Conversation.
    I. Title.
        HF5718.A37 2012
        658.4'52--dc23
                                                              2011036950

To the leaders of the world.

Acknowledgments

The most special thanks belong to my wife, Zaina, for her selfless love, her support, and her company during the preparation of this unique text.

Thank you also to my little daughter, Michèle, with whom I have shared so many special moments. Michèle, you are drop-dead gorgeous and you rock my world! You initiated me into fatherhood and you are the best thing that has ever happened to me.

I would like to thank Tom Carroll and Michelle Lara, who were always on call when I needed them. I am grateful for their guidance.

A very big acknowledgement goes to my developmental editor, Kirsten Dalley, for making the editing phase of this book so enjoyable, and for her tireless efforts on this project's behalf.

I would like to thank Lina and Bassam, both of whom have helped me get to this point.

No words should be wasted, and thanks to you, dear readers, hopefully mine have not been. I want to acknowledge you here, even if I don't know any of you by name.

Contents

Preface
13

How to Use This Book
15

Part 1
General Conversation
19

Part 2
At Work
41

Part 3
Conflicts and Anger
71

Part 4
Diplomacy
101

Part 5
Negotiation
119

Part 6
Problem Solving
133

Part 7
Courtesy
151

Part 8
Machiavellian Techniques
167

Bonus Section
181

Index
187

About the Author
191

Preface

Being thrust into an unpredictable situation can be extremely difficult, and this is doubly true when you are a leader. Regardless of whether you are an executive, a manager, a coach, a lawyer, a doctor, a politician, a salesperson, a diplomat, a den mother, or the head of a nation, you are expected to be able to take charge, influence the situation, settle the score, and make things better. This isn't always easy, and it can be especially stressful if you are fumbling for words and/or lacking in nuance in your communications. The fact that you reached for this book means that you probably aren't satisfied with the status quo. You know you can do better, but you need the magic phrases to help get you there. And because you are busy, you need a quick and easy guide to help you shine, both inside and outside of the office.

This book enumerates specific responses that have helped leaders and decision-makers like you shine. There is no other book out there like it. My goal in writing this book was to share these talking points so that you can develop a trustworthy, convincing leadership presence in *any* situation that life throws at you. In the past, rising executives used to spend time at seminars and conferences to gain the knowledge they needed to advance in their fields. The pace of business today has rendered this strategy largely out of date. The higher you move up the chain of command, the more readily you will need to be able to summon powerful and effective words and phrases—to motivate, to inspire, to command. Ideally they should become second nature, a part of your everyday routine. To help you do that, this book is organized into seven easy-to-digest sections, plus one bonus section at the end.

The fact is no matter how successful you are, chances are your speaking (and listening) skills could use some polishing and fine-tuning. This invaluable tool will enhance your command of the English language and allow your confidence and leadership skills to shine through. I can promise a rewarding experience, both personally and professionally, as you learn to speak boldly, persuasively, and, perhaps most of all, appropriately in any situation.

Let our journey to powerful communications begin!

How to Use
This Book

This book was designed with flexibility in mind. You can read it all the way through to get a general overview of the topic, or you can work on one particular situation or aspect of communication that you find the most challenging or relevant. For example, you may feel very comfortable addressing the public in challenging times, but not as relaxed handling conflicts with others. Use the Contents and the Index to help you find the area that is most applicable to your situation.

Read all the sample phrases and familiarize yourself with the ones that seem the most natural or comfortable for you. Then, practice them until they flow naturally from your mouth. When the time comes, you'll have no trouble summoning them and using them with confidence and aplomb. If you like, you can also add your own catch phrases in the margins; after all, everyone says things slightly differently. Remember that meaning is both expressed in and influenced by tone, body language, and timing (context). Thus, a humorous phrase that would be effective and appropriate in one setting could be construed as hostile and inappropriate in another, depending on how it is said, to whom you are speaking, and so on. So even though these phrases are "ready-to-use" in a certain sense, it is not a one-size-fits-all scenario. Use good judgment and let context be your guide. This is particularly important when you are considering using humor as a rhetorical device. Humor can sometimes come across as flip or dismissive, and not everyone will "get" your style. As always, nuance is required.

The visual accompanying each situation will help you anchor each "order of magnitude" in your mind, which will serve as a valuable mnemonic device down the road. For example, in the sample on page 17, the continuum indicator goes from **Conciliatory** to **Argumentative**. All of the phrases are sorted incrementally in terms of this scale. If you want to build bridges and smooth things over, learn and use the phrases toward the top. If you want to eliminate or ignore the niceties and cut to the chase, use the phrases toward the bottom.

Finally, I thought it important to note that I am not just working within the parameters of what is considered proper usage; thus, the reader will find colloquialisms and some slang. This is the English language as many people understand and use it in America. Obviously, the vagaries of expression will be much different in, say, Canada or Australia, or even in different parts of the States. Ultimately, our language, like all others, is a living thing. The field of linguistics is therefore in constant flux, with new words and idiomatic phrases continually being created, fine-tuned, modified, and, in some cases, eventually discarded. Therefore I'm prepared for the fact that the material in this book will need updating from time to time, as the way we express ourselves inevitably evolves. Please visit my Website, *www.patrickalain.com*, for the most up-to-date information to add to your linguistic arsenal. I also welcome your comments and criticisms of this work to help me in that process.

When Someone Is Picking a Fight

CONCILIATORY

ARGUMENTATIVE

- Clearly I have offended you; I am so sorry!
- I certainly did not mean to offend you.
- You seem really upset—what can I do to remedy the situation?
- Let's keep this professional.
- I would rather work this out in a more civil fashion.
- I really would rather not escalate this any further.
- You don't have to act this way, you know.
- There is still time to salvage this situation.
- A true professional puts his/her personal issues aside.
- You need to think about someone else besides yourself.
- Other people have feelings besides you, you know.
- You seem to be on the warpath today—I'd better stay out of your way.
- If you're looking for a fight, I'd be more than happy to oblige.
- If you are looking for trouble, you've found it!
- Boy, someone sure woke up on the wrong side of the bed.

General Conversation

A good conversationalist says what someone wants to remember.
—John Mason Brown

Speaking well is an important skill to master. When you speak, it is crucial to not only say the right thing, but to avoid common pitfalls. Here are six invaluable tips to help you speak like a leader:

1. Speak clearly and briefly

Ordinary people who aspire to be leaders should express their thoughts with clarity and brevity. No one likes someone who hogs a conversation or who speaks in circles and endless tangents. Donald Trump, CEO and chairman of The Trump Organization, is a good example of a clear speaker. He doesn't try to blind anyone with meaningless words, but rather comes right at you with straight talk. As he wrote in his book *How to Get Rich*, "[B.S.] will only get you so far." That is a clear thought in a few simple words. I couldn't have said it better myself!

2. Expand your vocabulary

Don't ever think that you have finally attained a great vocabulary. Make a commitment to learn one or two new words every day. Read magazines and books and underline words you don't know; learn their meanings and practice ways to include them in your everyday speech. If you know, say, a thousand more words than the average person, it will make you stand out from the crowd. You'll have the vocabulary of a leader.

3. Gain command of the idiom

Cultivate the nuances of your language and show them off. This is a process, not a goal. Whenever possible, incorporate colorful and vivid idiomatic phrases and terms—a "New York minute," "punch drunk love"—into your spoken shorthand (being careful to avoid clichés, of course). This will make your communications that much more memorable and persuasive.

4. Delegate your communications whenever possible

The higher leaders get in the organizational food chain, the more risk they assume. Much more is riding on every communication than when they were, say, working in the mail room or as a minion on the sales team. Their words can create a cascade of positive effects or get them crushed as flat as a flounder. They can make the top story on the evening news or the front page of a scandal rag. Their words can create comfort or bring despair. The impact of what they say increases exponentially with their visibility, which is why many corporate and political leaders delegate many of their external communications to their PR handlers. If you can do this, by all means take advantage of it.

5. Learn from others' mistakes

When you notice someone communicating poorly, first check yourself to make sure you aren't doing the same thing. Model exemplary communication habits to those around you and you'll naturally become better at it over time.

6. Back up your ideas with knowledge

Leaders tend to draw on personal anecdotes or their knowledge of current events and history to augment their arguments. For the biggest impact, focus on topical news items, recent sports results, new movie releases, or information you've gleaned from personal experience, and reference all of this in your conversations.

How to Agree

EFFUSIVE

- True!
- That's absolutely true.
- You're reading my mind.
- I couldn't agree more.
- I agree with you wholeheartedly.
- I agree.
- We're on the same page about this.
- That's a good point.
- I'm in complete agreement.
- That makes total sense.
- I know exactly what you mean.
- We see eye to eye.
- You're correct.
- My opinion corresponds with yours.
- Our opinions coincide very well.
- You've touched on the essence of what I was trying to say.
- Our thoughts are in complete accord.
- I'm in full agreement with you.
- I subscribe to your point of view.
- I think your point is very well taken.
- I'm glad to see that we're on the same page.
- Common sense tells me you're right.
- We're on the same wavelength.
- I'm square with you on that.
- I have no problem with that.
- Your view of things is well received.
- Your point has relevance.
- I have no qualms with your perception of things.
- I concede the point.
- I give up—you win.
- You're going to keep arguing until I give up, so have it your way.
- You're right, as always. [sarcasm]

BEGRUDGING

How to Disagree

CIVIL

BLUNT

- We appear to have a divergence of beliefs.
- I understand the point you're making, but...
- I certainly get what you're saying, but...
- I respect your point of view, but...
- I don't entirely agree with you on that.
- I must courteously disagree with you.
- I respectfully disagree.
- That's not the way I see it.
- That's one way to look at it, but it's not the right way.
- Few experts on this subject would agree with you.
- There's more than one way to look at this situation.
- There's a lot of speculating going on here.
- There's obviously a divergence in interpretation.
- I have a point of disagreement.
- I guess we're going to agree to disagree.
- I have great doubts about that.
- Not really, but I value your opinion.
- There's a better way to look at this.
- Your premise is a bit flawed.
- You might want to look it up because that's not right.
- You leave me no choice but to disagree with you.
- I don't subscribe to this point of view.
- I have no option but to disagree with you.
- Our opinions are radically different.
- My disagreement with you stems from the simple fact that you're wrong.
- I disagree with you completely.
- There is no truth to that whatsoever.
- You need more education on the matter.
- You're out of touch.
- You couldn't be more wrong.
- You're so wrong, you don't even know how wrong you are!

How to Open a Conversation

COURTEOUS

- It's great talking to you.
- I can't wait to get deeper into this topic with you.
- I've wanted to talk with you for a long time.
- I would appreciate having a conversation with you.
- I'd like to talk to you about something for a moment.
- Do you have a minute? I would like to discuss something with you.
- It would help me a lot to know your opinion on...
- I really want to have a dialogue with you about this.
- I'm listening to you and I want to understand.
- Today, I'm hoping we can discuss...
- Please feel free to speak openly.
- Whatever results from our discussions will be just fine.
- I'd like for our conversation to lead to something concrete.
- I've always been good with conversing freely—how about you?
- I'd like to elaborate a bit on...
- This is a tricky subject—let's talk about it for a while.
- Let's take a whack at this, shall we?
- At this point, the more we talk, the better it will be.
- I need to get my point across.
- We'll get further if we can get along from the start.
- My goal is for this to become less ambiguous.
- Please help me get comfortable with your side of the argument.
- Why not simply talk about it? What could be the harm in that?
- I'm not looking to simply talk—I'm in this to make something happen.

RUDE

- I'm seeing you today to hear you out and possibly help you.
- We should have started this discussion long ago.
- I wish we didn't have to talk about this, but there isn't any way around it.
- The only reason you're here is so I can hear you out.
- This is probably pointless, but let's see how far we can get.
- We may as well get going with this—I haven't got all day.
- I'm calling you out!
- Get in here and talk to me now!

How to Close a Conversation

PROFESSIONAL

- Talking to you is always a pleasure.
- I can't believe how wonderfully our talk went.
- This dialogue was very helpful, thank you.
- I learned a lot talking to you, thanks for everything.
- I'm sorry this is over—I was learning a lot.
- Thank you, I enjoyed our talk immensely.
- It was great talking to you.
- I got a lot out of our conversation.
- I apologize, but I must leave.
- I could listen to you for hours but, alas, I must go now.
- I'd like to continue with this, but I'm late for...
- I have pressing matters to attend to now.
- Let's stop here.
- Sorry, but I'm needed elsewhere.
- I regret I can't pursue this conversation any longer.
- Sorry, I prefer not to continue.
- This is as good a place to end our discussion as any.

UNPROFESSIONAL

- We won't be able to get anything out of such a big subject in just a day.
- I can't be of any use to you from this point on.
- Can we talk about something else, please?
- There's no need to discuss this any further.
- We've spoken enough about this.
- Let's stop this right here.
- Let's pull back before we go too far.
- This discussion isn't appropriate any longer.
- This topic disturbs me quite a bit.
- We could talk about it for 10 years and we still wouldn't have an answer.
- More talk would simply be a waste of our time.
- I just don't want to speak about this now.
- I'm not interested in this topic any more.
- As far as I'm concerned, this conversation is over.
- My apologies if I choose to not waste my time with this conversation. [sarcasm]
- Talking to you just makes my brain hurt.
- I'm not listening... [musically]
- I have nothing more to say to you.
- This conversation is over!
- You'd better shut your mouth before you put your foot in it.

How to Share News

GOOD

- This news is so good, it will blow your mind!
- This is such great news, there's no way to hide it!
- I can't wait to tell you this amazing news!
- This is what you've been waiting to hear!
- The best thing just happened—let me tell you about it!
- You won't believe the news I have for you!
- Wait until you hear this!

- I'm really pleased to tell you that...
- I can't do this news justice, but I'll try.
- This piece of information is going to make your day.
- I'm not sure how to say this, but...
- I think this is something you should know.
- I'm going to have to let you down easy.
- I'm afraid I have to give you the lowdown about...
- I'm going to have to break it down for you.
- Let me put this as gently as I can.
- I don't mean to bring you down, but...
- I didn't want to be the one to tell you this, but...
- Don't shoot the messenger, but...
- There's no good way to cut the deck, so let me just say...
- It's not easy to say what I'm about to say.
- I hate to be the bearer of bad tidings, but...
- You aren't going to like what I have to say, but...
- There's no good way to tell you this, but...
- Are you sitting down? I'm afraid I have news you probably don't want to hear.
- I'm afraid I have some bad news to report.
- Yes, it's bad—here's the scoop.

BAD

How to Express an Opinion

- I can say without equivocation that...
- With much conviction, I say...
- I'm speaking from experience when I say...
- There is no doubt in my mind that...
- I can assure you I know what I am talking about.
- There is no hesitation in what I am about to say.
- If you'll allow me to be frank.
- From my perspective...
- Let me just say...

CERTAIN

UNCERTAIN

- What I am trying to say is...
- It's just my gut feeling, but let me say...
- If you'll allow me to interject for a moment...
- That's all good, but what I am trying to say is...
- My guess would be...
- I feel I have to get this off of my chest.
- I think I'd like to say something here.
- If I am not mistaken...
- I'm not sure, but I think...
- I could be wrong, but...
- I may not have assurance, but...
- I know I'm usually wrong, but take this for what it's worth.
- May I add my measly two cents?

How to Ask for Someone's Opinion

POLITE

- I'd love to get your take on this.
- Is there anything you'd like to add?
- I welcome all opinions, so please speak freely.
- Would you like to interject?
- What do you think about...?
- I am open to any suggestions.
- Would you like contribute to this dialogue?
- What's your view of the situation?
- It would help me a lot to know your opinion on...
- As a proponent of [...], would you say that [...]?
- Dialogue is key—what do you have to say?
- Don't be afraid of being misunderstood.
- Please speak freely.
- Any input is welcome.
- If you don't agree, show me an alternative.

RUDE

- What's your best answer?
- I can't proceed without hearing from you.
- Speak your mind or forever hold your peace.
- Have you got an answer or not?
- You're going to say it anyway, so get it over with!
- Just spit it out already!

How to Express an Opinion

TACTFUL

- Let me put this as delicately as I can.
- While I think there may be more sides to this, let me begin by saying...
- Without making any concessions, I believe...
- Without choosing sides, let me say that...
- Although it's hard to put into words, I must admit that...
- Even before all the votes are counted, let me say that...
- Before the news comes in, I would like to acknowledge that...
- While all the ballots aren't in, I'd like to say that...
- I understand that this is a tricky/delicate/taboo topic, but...
- I'm on the side that says...
- I have to be honest with you and say...
- Please hear me out when I say...
- I would like to be frank, is that okay?
- I have to tell you this directly.
- I don't want to step on anybody's toes, but...
- Listen, please! I have something of importance to say.
- With all due respect, I feel that...
- Let's not beat around the bush, okay?
- There's no good way to say this, so I'm just going to say it.
- Let's stop with the niceties and get everything on the table, shall we?

TACTLESS

How to Ask for More Information

POLITE

- I'm probably being dense, but could you say more on this?
- I would like to know your position better.
- Would you be able to substantiate this?
- Can you elaborate on your position?
- Would you say that one more time, please?
- Would you please shed some light on this?
- I'm sorry, could you tell me more?
- May I ask you to expand on that?
- Your points are well taken, but there are a few things I still need clarified.
- I would like to have all the information—would you please elaborate?
- Perhaps you could clear something up for me.
- I'm not sure what I heard—do you mind repeating it?
- Would you explain this a bit more thoroughly?
- Your message was a bit garbled—would you restate it?
- I may have misunderstood you—would you repeat that again?
- I'm not sure I understood you very well.
- Show me what you mean.
- Can you provide more information?
- I don't understand you at all. Would you clarify?
- Can you explain yourself more clearly?
- Sorry, what was your point?
- What are you trying to say?
- Is there something you're not telling me?
- Please get to the point.
- I need more than this to continue our discussion.
- Lay your cards on the table where I can see them.
- I demand an answer.
- Just spill the beans already!

RUDE

How to Clarify Your Point

DIPLOMATIC

- Let me word that a bit differently.
- I'm sorry, let me say it another way.
- I've got a few pointers that might help you out.
- Allow me to rephrase.
- This is a complicated issue; let's see if we can figure it out together.
- I have a few ideas that may help you understand better.
- This is a bit confusing, but I'm sure we can figure it out.
- Let's try to make sense of this.
- I can help you comprehend that better.
- I'll rephrase the information so it is more easily understood.
- Let me help you understand.
- If there are any misunderstandings, let's take care of them now.
- If anything is unclear, I'd like to deal with it.
- Let me be clear.
- Let's go over it again, for clarity's sake.
- I sense that we have a problem communicating—let's get this straightened out.
- I can repeat myself if you don't get it.
- If you don't understand, let me clarify.
- Let me try to make sense of it for you.
- If you're having trouble understanding, I can go over it again.
- I can make that clearer if you really need help understanding.
- If you don't understand, I guess you'll need to do some research.
- Don't guess when I can easily set you straight.
- I guess I'd better clarify what you can't seem to grasp.
- Let me make clear what you clearly don't comprehend.
- You're clearly out of your depth, so let me enlighten you.
- You're hopeless!

RUDE

How to Confide in Someone

TRUSTING

UNTRUSTING

- I feel like I could tell you anything.
- I have to be honest—you are the only one I trust.
- You are my sole confidant.
- You're the only one I can really talk to.
- I know I don't have to hold back when we speak.
- You're my go-to guy/girl.
- I put a lot of stock in your opinion.
- There are very few people I confide in.
- I trust you implicitly.
- I know I can rely on you to be discreet.
- I feel comfortable discussing this with you.
- I wouldn't say this if I didn't have faith in you.
- This is just between me and you.
- Trust is very important to me.
- After knowing each other for so long, I know I can trust you.
- To tell you the truth...
- My word is my bond.
- Can you keep a secret?
- I can tell you anything, right?
- What I tell you here, stays here.
- I have to disclose something to you, but I'm not sure if I should.
- I just want to confirm that these conversations are completely confidential.
- There are some things you must keep to yourself.
- What I'm about to tell you dies here.
- If you tell this to anyone, our relationship is over.

How to Change the Topic

CONSTRUCTIVE

- With the greatest respect for the agenda, I would like to also discuss this.
- Because of recent events/updates, I would like to prioritize a few additional points.
- Without conceding any points, I would like to address this side issue for a moment.
- We should look to the future now and discuss other ideas.
- Let's move on to something else—we have a lot to cover.
- Let's move on to the next point on the agenda.
- Let's not dwell on this too long.
- Do you mind if we change the subject?
- For the sake of everybody's time, let's move on.
- Can we move on? Everyone's time is valuable.
- I think we've thoroughly exhausted the topic—what's next?
- By the way, do you have any big plans for the weekend?
- I'd like to go to the movies—have you seen any good ones recently?
- Nice weather we're having, isn't it?
- Wouldn't you rather be talking about something else?
- Can we please talk about something else?
- Let's not dwell on this unnecessarily.
- I don't think it's constructive to continue discussing this.
- Actually, I'd rather talk about anything else but this.
- Please let's not persist with that.
- Why do you feel it's necessary to drone on about this?
- Let's not beat a dead horse, okay?
- Can't we put this topic aside?

DESTRUCTIVE

- This isn't a subject that can be solved right now, so let's not even try.
- Talking about this is like being up a river without a paddle—let's move on.
- We're talking in circles.
- Let's move on, please?
- Please, let's stop talking about this.
- If you keep hammering this incessantly, I just might scream.

How to Express Doubts

HIGH ROAD

- It seems to me that...
- I am not positive, but I think that...
- I am under the impression that...
- I don't think it's common knowledge, but...
- I have the feeling that...
- I'm having second thoughts about this.
- Something doesn't add up here.
- It seems that something is missing, but I can't quite put my finger on it.
- I am a bit skeptical about that.
- I'm not sure I understand what you mean.
- I am not 100-percent positive about that.
- There's a lot about this that I'm not sure of.
- The numbers just don't add up here.
- Where did you come up with that conclusion?
- I'm not confident in your sources.
- I'm not trying to insult you; I just have my doubts.
- I won't belabor the point because I don't think it's true.
- I have my doubts about what was just said.
- Do you really know or just think you know?

LOW ROAD

- I don't know what you're aiming at here.
- There's no certainty to that.
- I'm unsure about a lot of this
- I have a sinking feeling about this.
- Something is rotten in the State of Denmark.
- Where did you get *that* idea?
- I've seen clearer thinking from a kindergartner.
- Okay, whatever you say. [sarcasm]
- After reviewing your [work/plan/operation/idea], it's a wonder you can even tie your shoes. [sarcasm]

How to Reconnect With Someone You've Had a Falling-Out With

COURTEOUS

- I've missed our relationship; I'm so glad we worked things out!
- It's so nice to be working together/hanging out with you again.
- It's good to restore our relationship and move forward.
- I am glad this relationship is back on track.
- I know you're busy, so I understand if you missed my last e-mail.
- I'm so glad we're back together. I've missed our conversations so much.
- The both of us have been so busy; it's nice to be in touch again!
- Let's take a few minutes to catch up now that I have you back on the line.
- I'm sorry we grew apart—it was never my intention.
- There's a lot of water under the bridge—can we agree to start over?

RUDE

- I'm happy to resolve any issues we've had in the past and look forward to the future.
- Let's reconnect now that I have your phone number/e-mail address again.
- Let's get together and discuss what we've missed out on.
- I'm sorry, I guess I just got too busy/overwhelmed to deal with everything.
- I hope you can take a few minutes to catch me up on what you've been doing.
- I feel that you and I somehow got lost in translation.
- We should reconcile and talk things over.
- Let's let bygones be bygones and start over.
- We need to get together again and talk things out.
- You and I clearly fell through the cracks—it's hard to understand why.
- We should have never lost touch.
- I'm willing to let it go if you are.
- The ball is in your court now.
- Let's just move on already!

When You've Answered a Question

COURTEOUS

- Did that answer your question?
- Was that what you needed from me?
- Was that the kind of answer you were looking for?
- Was that answer satisfying?
- I'm glad I was able to provide a good answer.
- Did that make any sense?
- Are you following my train of thought?
- Thanks for listening; that definitely wasn't a short answer!
- That was a long answer; thanks for your patience.

- If I wasn't clear enough, please let me know.
- Were you able to grasp what I was saying?
- If you didn't understand everything, I would be glad to go over it again.
- If you didn't catch all of that, I could go over it again.
- Hmm, someone wasn't listening!
- What part of the answer didn't you get?
- Am I being clear or not?
- I can't help it if you didn't understand me.
- I don't have time for more details; time is money.
- That was my answer—take it or leave it.
- That's all I'm saying—I really could care less what you think/how you interpret it.

RUDE

When You Don't Want to Answer a Question

DIPLOMATIC

- There's probably no easy answer to that.
- There is more than one way to look at that.
- There's no straightforward answer to what you're asking.
- Let me think on that and get back to you.
- I just don't know what to say.
- Sorry, words escape me at the moment.
- I don't know enough to give a definitive answer either way.
- There isn't a simple answer to that question.
- There are no simple explanations.
- There's more than one school of thought, so I can't take a hard stand.
- This is a specialized topic and I'm certainly no expert.
- I think that it's arguable.
- I don't have enough information to give you an intelligent/informed answer.
- I don't know all the details about that.
- That could take hours to explain.
- I'm not sure, so perhaps it's best not to answer at this time.

- You would need specialized knowledge to understand.
- The answer is complicated, and honestly, you probably wouldn't understand anyway.
- It's quite technical; I'm not sure you have the knowledge to understand.
- As much as I'd love to spend time on this issue, I can't.
- The question is so important, I want to take some time before answering.
- I'd rather not answer that right now.
- I don't wish to enter into this conversation.
- I am not proficient enough to answer.
- This is outside my area of expertise.
- I have a tough time talking about this—let's move on to something else.
- I have no opinion on the matter.
- I make a rule never to speak about this with my friends/family/coworkers.
- I prefer to not talk about it.
- I prefer to stay out of this conversation.
- If I had something to say about this, I certainly wouldn't say it here.
- Your question isn't important in times like these.
- As much as I would love to spend time on this issue, I can't.
- I don't want to insult your intelligence, but this isn't as simple as you think.
- When you respect someone, you don't ask such questions.
- I can neither confirm nor deny that.
- I decline to comment.
- I plead the Fifth.
- You'll need to ask someone else.
- Beats me!

UNMANNERED

When You Are Asked to Repeat Yourself

COMPLIANT

- No problem; I'd be happy to!
- Gladly!
- I'm sorry if I went too fast/spoke too softly—I'll gladly say it again.
- Yes, the acoustics here are terrible. [joking]
- I'd like to reiterate that...
- I'll say it once more.
- I'll say it a thousand times if you need me to.
- I don't mind repeating myself, as long as it makes things clearer.
- I'm willing to elaborate if that's what you need.
- You obviously didn't hear me correctly—here's what I said.
- Does anyone have a microphone?
- Once more, with feeling.
- It isn't my habit to repeat myself, but obviously it's necessary.
- You can wait for the transcript if you want.
- I'll say it again, even though we're wasting everyone's time.
- I apologize; I don't have time to go over this again.
- Perhaps we can go into that again some other time/later/afterward.
- Sorry, there's no time to repeat myself.
- The acoustics here are so bad, I doubt that repeating myself will do any good.
- I'm afraid that restating my position will only serve to confuse the issue.
- I won't say it again because it's only going to hold things up.
- Everything I just said was crystal clear and doesn't need repeating.
- Doing that would be inconsiderate of the others.
- If you had listened in the first place, I wouldn't have to repeat myself.

RUDE

- You should have been listening more closely when I said it the first time.
- I told you enough about what I think.
- I'm only going to say this once more, so pay attention this time.
- Saying it again is completely unnecessary.
- Please remove the wax from your ears.
- Repetition is my greatest ally, it seems. [sarcasm]
- Are you deaf?

P
A
R
T

2

At Work

Great work is done by people who are not afraid to be great.
—Fernando Flores

Good communication in the workplace is just as crucial for the success of a low-level employee as it is for someone in management. However, for those who aspire to move up the corporate food chain, learning how to speak like a leader becomes even more important. Here are a few tips for anyone—whether entry level grunt or C-level honcho—to keep in mind:

1. Speak positively

Staying positive is one of the most important criteria for promotion. People who can put things in a positive light are proactive and tend to be well liked by their colleagues. Even while discussing a potentially negative topic, a positive speaker will always attempt to come up with solutions. Contrast this with the person who simply reports the negative situation without providing any helpful hints or strategies to deal with it. This kind of person will almost certainly be seen as a whiner or complainer—not exactly leadership material!

2. Think before you speak

Thinking of what you're going to say ahead of time is essential. Who hasn't made the mistake of jumping in and speaking too hastily, and harmed someone or revealed confidential information in the process? Crafting your thoughts before you open your mouth will prevent you from saying things that you regret or don't mean (politicians make this mistake all the time). The French have an expression for this: *Tourner sept fois sa langue dans sa bouche* ("Roll your tongue seven times in your mouth before you speak").

3. Finish each thought before moving on

The pace of business has never been faster, so most people have the tendency to go off half cocked and rush through subjects without finishing. By slowing down and wrapping up each topic before moving on, you will present yourself as a thoughtful and measured person. This approach will also make your colleagues feel more involved in what's going on.

4. Prepare your speeches

A good speaker recognizes that preparation for a speech is often more important than the speech itself. Flesh out the outline of each presentation in advance, grouping your thoughts in a logical hierarchy. Index cards are a great way to do this because they can be easily sorted and moved around. If you feel uncomfortable with public speaking (as many people do), you can rehearse the presentation in front of friends and family. A good rehearsal confirms that the content, language, and pacing are all in place and ready to go. With every speech, always start with summarizing the presentation and announcing how long it is going to last. Finally, always finish on a positive note.

5. Write like a leader

Whenever you put your thoughts down in writing, regardless of whether it is in a letter, an e-mail, or a blog post, be sure to follow these guidelines:

- Keep your target audience in mind. Be clear but not overly formal—unless you are writing to the Queen. Seek common ground with your reader(s) and it won't fail you.
- Pay attention to proper grammar, syntax, and mechanics. Yes, you can use shorthand in text messages to your spouse, for example, but in official correspondence, your words convey your image and, as such, they need to be spelled correctly.
- Formatting matters. To provide greater clarity and understanding, use bullet points, different typefaces, boldface, italics, and underlining judiciously.

How to Ask for a Raise

PROFESSIONAL

- Could you please take a moment and review my current level of compensation?
- My salary hasn't changed since I began working here. Can we look into that?
- I've taken on additional responsibility but don't have the salary to show for it.
- We're a much smaller team than when I started, so I need a raise to compensate.
- I did some research and I'm not making anything close to my current market value.
- It's been more than a year since I had a salary review.
- I think my work is the best it has ever been, but I'm still making the same salary.
- Can we at least discuss a cost of living adjustment?
- I can't think of any reason why I should be making the same money, can you?
- Let's discuss what needs to happen in order for me to get a raise.
- A raise won't get rid of the stress, but it sure will help me feel better.
- Everyone else is making more than I am; I hope we can discuss that.
- My salary needs an upward adjustment.
- I'm due a performance review *and* a raise. When can we make than happen?
- I don't think a raise would be unwarranted, given all I do here.

CONFRONTATIONAL

- I'm doing the work of two people. I simply need more money.
- I think I deserve a raise, and I won't be happy unless you agree.
- If you are happy with my work, you need to show that to me in concrete terms.
- I'm going to quit unless I get a salary adjustment.
- Either give me a raise or I quit.
- I can't take this job anymore; if I stay I'll need to make more money.
- If I don't get a raise right now, I'm walking out.

How to Ask for Time Off

CALM

- If it's okay with you I'd like to discuss taking some time off.
- I was thinking of taking a vacation—do these dates work for you?
- Would this be a good time to request some time off?
- What form do I need to fill out to request vacation?
- What form did you fill out when you went on vacation last month?
- If there is a standard vacation request, I'd like to fill one out.
- I'm having a family emergency so I'll need to take a week off.
- A sudden emergency has come up; I need a week off to tend to it.
- A family member has passed away and I need bereavement leave.
- I'm going to have a baby so I'll need to request some maternity leave.

CONFRONTATIONAL

- I've been having some medical problems so I will need to take some of my sick leave.
- How long do I have to be on the job before I qualify for time off?
- Because of all the stress lately I need to schedule a mental health break.
- I deserve a vacation. Can you tell me how to request one?
- Most people who have worked here this long get time off; I think I should, too.
- I don't see why I can't take some vacation time. I've earned it.
- Just wanted to give you a heads-up: I'm going on vacation on these dates.
- The only question I have is, should I take one week off or two?
- I don't believe I'm at the level where I need to ask permission to take some time off.
- I've earned some time off and I'm going to take it, no matter what you say.

How to Say No to Your Boss

DIPLOMATIC

- Okay, but which of these tasks do you want me to finish first?
- What about the other three tasks you've given me?
- I wish I could help with this but I am tapped out at the moment.
- Is there someone else you could call on? I have so many plates in the air right now!
- If I say yes I'm afraid my work quality will suffer.
- I can't imagine taking on that much responsibility, sorry.

- I wish I had five heads but I'm only one person, I'm afraid.
- I'm not sure that your request is entirely reasonable, given how hard we are all working.
- Two people used to do that job—can one person really do it alone?
- I'd be happy to, as long as my salary is adjusted to reflect the additional workload.
- Can we look into hiring someone else/an assistant?
- I don't think it's right for you to pile all this work on me.
- It may be within your authority to ask me to do that, but I don't think it's a smart move.
- That's not in my pay grade/part of my job description/something I am going to do.
- Maybe you should handle that yourself.
- Do you think *you* could handle that much work?
- You've exceeded your boundaries, and I'd like you to stop.
- I am going to have to object to being treated like a robot/slave.
- This is completely out of bounds and I'm not going to stand for it.
- It's unfair to ask something of your employee that you're not willing to do yourself.
- I'd rather not.
- I am not your slave.
- You're not the boss of me.

BLUNT

How to Avoid Talking About a Personal Issue

POLITE

BLUNT

- I'm up to my neck right now—can we talk later?
- Can we meet after work to discuss this?
- I'm sorry, but I'd just rather not talk about that.
- That's kind of a sore subject for me, sorry.
- That's just too upsetting/personal/close to home, sorry.
- I'm just not comfortable talking about that at work.
- This is probably not the best time or place to talk about this.
- Maybe we should talk about this later.
- I think other people can overhear us—let's talk later.
- I'm under the gun today. Maybe we can talk at lunch.
- I feel this is a bit too personal to talk about at work, don't you?
- That's simply too personal to address here.
- I don't feel like talking about that.
- I prefer to keep my private life private.
- That's not something I like to discuss at work.
- Do I look like I have the time to talk about this?
- I prefer to keep my work life and private life separate.
- There's no reason to bring that up.
- When did I ever give you the impression that it was okay to talk about this?
- Wow, this is *so* not appropriate.
- Sure, *you're* the person I would want to discuss this with. [sarcasm]

How to Bring Up a Personal or Embarrassing Issue

POLITE

BLUNT

- May I tell you something in confidence?
- I don't know who else to turn to—can we talk for a moment?
- May I close the door? I have something personal I need to share.
- I've got something to share that's fairly private. Do you have a moment?
- I really need to talk to you about something.
- This is most unpleasant, but I really appreciate your tact and discretion.
- Admittedly this is kind of personal, but I think you can handle it.
- I know this is embarrassing, but I know I can trust you.
- Something's come up that I need to talk to you about.
- Ugh, I need to confide in you for a moment.
- This may be a little personal, but I consider you a friend.
- I've never needed to talk this badly. Do you have a minute?
- You're the only person here who will understand.
- Please keep this under your hat when I tell you.
- I'm going to tell you something but you need to keep it a secret.
- There's never a good time or place to discuss this, so I'm just going to say it.
- What I tell you here dies here, okay?
- This is pretty embarrassing—you sure you wanna hear about it?
- I know this is inappropriate, but...
- I hope this isn't TMI, but...
- Yuck, wait until you hear this.

How to Boost Someone's Confidence

EFFUSIVE

- You're so good at what you do, I should be fearful of losing *my* job!
- How did I ever get anything done before you arrived?
- Is there nothing you can't do?
- I know I never have to worry about your work.
- I have complete confidence in your abilities.
- You were born to do this.
- You're the perfect person for this job.
- I know you can do it.
- You are among the best workers here.
- Your ability to get things done is admirable.
- Everyone knows how capable you are.
- You have a real talent for this.
- You can make this your best work ever.
- Everyone knows how good you are.
- You can do no wrong here.
- You haven't disappointed me yet.
- When have you ever dropped the ball?
- You're my best choice at the moment.
- I know you can move mountains if you put your mind to it.
- I know you're equal to the task.
- This is the time to really make it count.
- Here's your chance to show us what you're made of.
- You've done more challenging tasks in the past.
- Don't worry about it—you know you're good.
- People have told me you're good, so don't let them down
- What's important is that you believe in yourself.

MEASURED

How to Ask for a Private Conversation

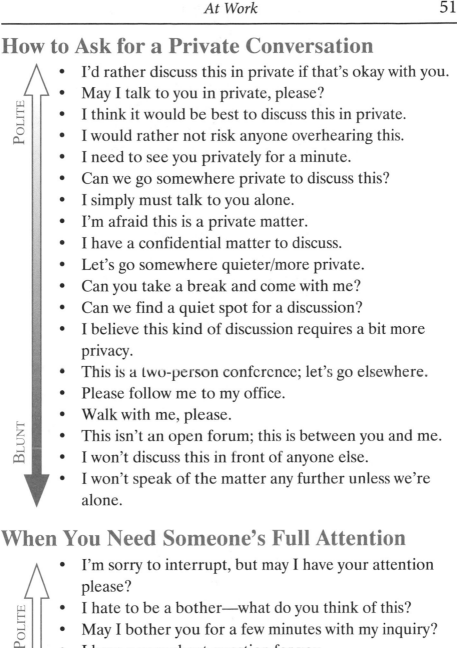

POLITE

- I'd rather discuss this in private if that's okay with you.
- May I talk to you in private, please?
- I think it would be best to discuss this in private.
- I would rather not risk anyone overhearing this.
- I need to see you privately for a minute.
- Can we go somewhere private to discuss this?
- I simply must talk to you alone.
- I'm afraid this is a private matter.
- I have a confidential matter to discuss.
- Let's go somewhere quieter/more private.
- Can you take a break and come with me?
- Can we find a quiet spot for a discussion?
- I believe this kind of discussion requires a bit more privacy.
- This is a two-person conference; let's go elsewhere.
- Please follow me to my office.
- Walk with me, please.
- This isn't an open forum; this is between you and me.
- I won't discuss this in front of anyone else.

BLUNT

- I won't speak of the matter any further unless we're alone.

When You Need Someone's Full Attention

POLITE

- I'm sorry to interrupt, but may I have your attention please?
- I hate to be a bother—what do you think of this?
- May I bother you for a few minutes with my inquiry?
- I have a very short question for you.
- I must go over some crucial points with you.
- Do I have your full attention?
- Can you hear me okay?
- I'm not sure if I have your full attention.

BLUNT

- This is important—please pay attention.
- I'm explaining important things to you.
- I think you'll hear me better if you pay attention.
- You don't seem very attentive to what I'm saying
- You're clearly not focusing on what I'm saying.
- I'm explaining things to you and you don't seem to be listening.
- I'm sorry, but you seem a little distracted.
- I feel like I'm not being heard.
- Am I not getting through to you?
- I'm not sure you're listening attentively to me
- Listen up—what I have to say is very important.
- Will you please pay attention for a minute?
- Are you at all interested in what I'm saying?
- Do I always have to ask you to listen to me?
- Are you even aware that I'm talking to you?
- I feel like I'm talking to myself, here.
- I have the feeling that you're not very interested.
- Are you even a tiny bit interested in what I'm saying?
- Am I speaking to the wall, here?
- Please look at me when I'm talking to you.
- Let me know when you can give me five minutes of your time.
- Talking to you is a waste of my time.
- I could communicate better with a rock.
- Cleaning your ears might help. [sarcasm]
- Hello, is anybody home? [sarcasm]
- Did someone forget their ADD meds?

How to Assign a Task to Someone

POLITE

- Would you be so kind as to...
- Do you want to do it, or would you like me to?
- Would you like to step in, here?
- I have an opportunity you may be interested in.

- Is there any way you could take care of this?
- Are you open to the idea of additional work?
- Will you please help me out?
- Would you take a few seconds to...?
- Are you available to take on something new?
- Would you please handle this for me?
- Would you do me a favor, please?
- I have something to ask of you that shouldn't take too long.
- Would you look into this new assignment, please?
- Would you mind...?
- This won't take but a moment.
- It would mean a lot to me if you took this on.
- I have a heavy responsibility to delegate.
- Here is one more task to add to your list.
- Care to take a crack at it?
- I'll pay you a bonus if...
- If you can handle this, there's a little extra money/a promotion in it for you.
- The following needs to be done by [date].
- Can I trust you to...?
- We need to have this done by [date].
- I expect you to have this finished by...
- Do I always have to ask you to do things that need to be done?
- I suggest you take on more responsibility here.
- Do you mean that you haven't done it already?
- Wasn't this due yesterday?
- I'm waiting... [sarcasm]
- I'm not asking you to do this, I'm telling you.
- I guess there's always the option of feeling the door hitting you on the way out.

BLUNT

How to Call a Meeting to Order

PROFESSIONAL

- Would everyone be so kind as to take their seats?
- I've gathered everyone here to talk about something very critical.
- Please, everyone take your seats.
- Let's get down to business, shall we?
- Let's go over the purpose for our meeting today.
- Let's open this up for debate.
- Here's our order of business for today.
- Our agenda for today's meeting is...
- Let me call this meeting to order.
- The reason we're here today is...
- Let's begin this by first outlining our order of business.
- If you have your notepads ready, let's get started.
- It's time to start, so please give me your undivided attention.
- The topic(s) for this session is...
- Let's dig right into the subject of today's meeting.
- I'd be happy if we could tackle the complex issues first.
- Let's start by going over what we want to accomplish today.
- I think we all know why we're here today.
- We can't begin without first knowing what we hope to accomplish.
- If we can't get started, we'll have to do it all over again tomorrow.
- The longer we put this off, the longer we'll have to stay here.
- If I have to light a fire under you to get this started, I will. [joking]

CASUAL

- Let's get a move on and start the meeting already.
- Can we just hold this meeting, please?
- Can we just begin already?
- Time is money, people!
- I'm growing old waiting for you guys to settle down.
- I'd like to begin sometime during this century. [sarcasm]

How to Terminate a Meeting

PROFESSIONAL

- With your concurrence, I think we're at a good point to adjourn for the day.
- Thank you for coming and being a part of this important meeting.
- I think we can all feel good about what we accomplished today.
- It seems that we've covered everything we needed to— let's call it a day, shall we?
- Let's come back to this when we reconvene next week/ month/year.
- Let's disperse and think about everything we've talked about.
- Congratulations on a job well done, everyone.
- Everything turned out quite well, I think.
- I think we've done enough for today, don't you?
- Let's table the other items until next time.
- We aren't getting anywhere, so let's stop for today.
- If this goes on much longer, we are all just going to mentally check out.
- These talks are no longer accomplishing anything.
- Let's call it quits for today, okay?

UNMANNERED

- Let's give it a rest.
- I'm done with this meeting.
- This meeting is so over!
- I'm out of here!
- I feel happy hour coming on—who's with me?
- It must be 5 o'clock somewhere!

How to Refocus a Conversation

POSITIVE

- I always want to encourage new ideas, but let's stay on track.
- That's very true, but let's get back to where we were.
- I hear what you're saying, but for now let's keep on topic.
- I like the way you think, but let's continue where we left off.
- Let's stay focused on the task at hand.
- I think we're getting a little off track here.
- As you may recall, the purpose of this meeting was...
- We have to remember that the purpose of this meeting is...
- The essence of the topic is still...
- I think we should take a few steps back and finish the original discussion.
- Let's stay on track for now.
- It's a shame if we let the essentials slip through our fingers.
- Let's not turn onto a dead end.
- Let's not get lost in trivialities/tangents.
- We're not staying focused here.
- We would all benefit if we stayed focused.
- Let's stay on point, please.
- I think we're getting distracted from the real issue.

NEGATIVE

- We don't need to take these talks in a different direction.
- We're moving further and further off track.
- We've managed to completely go off topic; let's start over.
- That is a whole topic unto itself.
- We are completely missing the point now.
- I'm tired of all the tangents.
- That is totally besides the point!

How to Propose an Action or Solution

PASSIVE

- This may not work, but what if we did X?
- I could be way off, but what if we tried X?
- If I may, I'd like to propose that we do X.
- I'd like to get your thoughts on this proposal.
- What would the group think if we did X?
- Can we discuss the pros and cons of X?
- I've got a possible solution that may or may not fit the bill.
- I may have an answer to that question.
- We need to explore all avenues, but here's one idea...
- There's more than one way to skin a cat; here's what I think...
- There are several possible answers to this; here is but one example...
- Maybe we can look at the problem from a different perspective.
- Experts seem to think that...
- Other people have done X in this situation.
- I've got a way to move forward; let me explain.
- I've seen problems like this before, and I suggest...
- I have arrived at what I believe is a workable solution.
- We need to find a solution to this mess; here is what I propose...

ASSERTIVE

- After much consideration, I believe the best course of action would be to...
- I think we need to focus on the next logical step, which is...
- I submit that the following will be necessary.
- I think the time has come for us to do X.
- There's no way we can avoid doing X.
- Here's what we're going to do.
- This is the only possible solution and that's final
- I haven't heard a better solution yet, have you?
- There is no alternative but to do this.
- Either you're with me or you're against me.

How to Put Off a Task

CIVIL

- I wish I could address this, but I'm completely tapped out right now.
- I'm swamped right now—can we revisit this some other time?
- I'd be delighted to set aside time to go over this [next week/month/year].
- It will be my pleasure to get back to you about that on [specific time].
- If you can hold off for a bit, I'll take care of it on [specific time].
- I'll get back to it when I'm free I promise.
- Sorry to put you off, but I just can't give this task the time it deserves right now.
- I can't prioritize this right now. Is it okay that I take care of it some other time?
- Unfortunately, I'll have to delay.
- I may have time to work on this later but I can't promise anything.

- I understand that this is very important, but it's not my priority right now.
- You'll have to come back some other time.
- Why don't we let that go for now?
- We'll deal with that some other time.
- This will be dealt with when I have the time.
- Well, you don't manage my calendar, do you?
- I'm not dealing with your request today, but I'll let you know if and when I do.
- You're being unreasonable—now is not the time.
- I don't even have a second to entertain your request.
- Ask me next week if I care.
- Yeah, *that's* gonna happen! [sarcasm]

BLUNT

How to Defer a Conversation

POLITE

- I'd be delighted to set aside time for this on [insert specific time].
- I would prefer if we discussed this at a later date.
- We'll cover more about this at a later time.
- Let's push this discussion until [insert specific time].
- Let me get up to speed and we'll chat [insert specific time].
- The question/issue deserves some serious thought—let's revisit this when we know more.
- I'd be more comfortable if we could talk when I'm less distracted/busy/tired—how about [insert specific time]?
- I'll send you an e-mail and address that in greater depth.
- I'm going to need to think about this and get back to you.
- I need to go over this in my head first.
- I will need to learn more about the topic before we talk.
- We'll talk about it when it becomes necessary, but not before.

RUDE

- Let me get back to you on that.
- Let me think about it.
- Let's push this discussion to [insert specific time/date].
- I don't think this is the best time to talk about this.
- I have nothing to add right now—we'll talk about it again, I'm sure.
- We'll have to talk some other time.
- Let's revisit this some other time, okay?
- Do we have to talk about this right now?
- Continuing this conversation today is out of the question.
- I *said* we'd do it another time.
- I can't handle this right now.
- There's no way I can listen to you now.
- You're crazy if you think I'm going to talk to you about this now.
- Stop bothering me—I'll talk about it when I'm good and ready.

How to Postpone a Decision

POLITE

- Only fools rush in—let's think on this some more.
- Let's take our time to find the right solution rather than rush to a mistake.
- Let's take some time and think about what we want to accomplish here.
- We don't need to make a decision right this very moment.
- Let's sleep on it first, okay?
- I think we should get some distance on this before we decide.
- Let's table this until later.
- I think we can make this judgment later.

RUDE

- I'll definitely think about it and get back to you.
- When do you need an answer to this?
- Let me get back to you with my verdict.
- We can come back to this issue in the future.
- This decision may require further analysis.
- Let's think about what we really want and get back to it later.
- We're not making any progress—let's talk about it later.
- We should work on this when the dust has settled.
- I don't think now is the time discuss this.
- I think we could all benefit from a cooling off period.
- We will discuss this later.
- We'll talk about it when the time comes.
- I will not bow to the tyranny of the urgent.
- I'm not going to give my decision right now, and that's final!

How to Unite People

INSPIRING

- Only by working with one another will we succeed.
- We'll be unstoppable if we have a common vision.
- We can overcome any obstacle if we work together toward a common goal.
- Raise your hand if you're a team player!
- Once we agree, nothing will stop us.
- We're all happiest when our goals are one and the same.
- Tomorrow's page—no one can write it alone.
- Together, we are stronger than we are as individuals.
- A strand of three [or 20, or 200] is not easily broken.
- The bonds that hold us are stronger than the forces that separate us.

INTIMIDATING

- How we deal with these changes now will make or break our future.
- Let's work together and move forward.
- I think we can all agree that...
- Together, we can take the high road and succeed.
- I'd like to see you join with me in solving this issue.
- Let's all look at the big picture.
- Let's proceed in a spirit of togetherness.
- The good of the company should be our common goal.
- We will succeed if we work as one unit.
- I know you all have the capacity to work together, but now you need to show me.
- We'll get this done faster if we all work together.
- A common goal will help head off problems down the road.
- United we stand, divided we fall.
- Infighting and power plays will get you nowhere.
- This is no place for fence-sitters or the partially committed.
- The collective takes precedence over the individual here.
- We either stay together, or you get out of the way.
- We don't tolerate dissent within our ranks.

How to Flatter a Superior

EFFUSIVE

- I worship the ground you walk on—is that wrong?
- I put you up on a pedestal.
- This is easily the best [report/briefing/analysis/work] that I've ever seen.
- The way you do X is simply amazing!
- I'm amazed at how you handle everything.
- I love watching you in action.
- I learn so much from you every day.

- Your work sets you apart from everyone else.
- I am inspired by your determination/work ethic/will to succeed.
- I'm proud to be on your team/working for you.
- Men/women of talent *and* integrity are rare.
- I shouldn't go on so much about your work, but I can't help myself.
- This could be the beginning of a beautiful partnership.
- With results like these, you'll be unstoppable.
- With your discipline, you won't be staying in the mail room forever. [joking]
- It's good to be on board with you and your team.
- If I worked as hard as you, I would have made partner by now.
- Your achievements speak volumes about your dedication
- You deserve every accolade you receive.
- Everybody should put as much gusto in their work as you do.
- If everyone worked as hard as you, this company would be ahead of the game.
- Once again, you make us all look bad. [joking]
- Nice work, as usual.
- Not too shabby, partner!

SUBTLE

How to Motivate an Employee

- You are wonderful to work with—keep it up!
- I can see your bonus/raise/promotion from here!
- Keep up the great work—it won't go unnoticed.
- Never, ever, ever give up!
- There's no time like the present to kick it into high gear.

POSITIVE

- I'm right behind you, encouraging you with each step forward.
- You are *so* close to the finish line!
- I am proud of you—keep up the good work.
- When we work as a team we always get great results.
- Now isn't the time to stop—let's press on to the end.
- You can become one of the elite if you put your mind to it.
- Hard times will soon be a thing of the past if you hang in there.
- Even the longest journey begins with a single step.
- Keep your eyes on the prize.
- It comes down to a single question: What future do you want to create?
- You are the employee you decide to become.
- Just how committed are you to making this job work?
- You need to keep your nose to the grindstone
- Our company's future is in your hands—don't drop the ball.
- I can see the light at the end of the tunnel, and it isn't an oncoming train. [joking]
- We're making some progress, but we're still not there yet.
- You need to work smarter, not necessarily harder.
- The job won't get done if you don't pull your weight.
- The only place to go from here is up.
- The company is expecting more from you—I hope you're up for it.
- I'm sure you will do better next time.
- We are watching you every moment of every day.
- I don't want to hear myself talking; I want progress.
- You either cut the mustard or you're done.

NEGATIVE

When an Employee Is Underperforming

GENTLE

- Is your work load too stressful? Maybe I can help.
- Is there something on your mind? Something you'd like to discuss?
- Are you having any issues away from work? You seem distracted/unhappy/disengaged.
- Your work quality has been suffering as of late—what can we do to turn it around?
- Perhaps you need a little break to regroup.
- I know you are capable of much more than this.
- You need to carry your weight in order to get the recognition you deserve.
- You have such potential—why are failing to follow through?
- I know you've got a lot more talent than what I've been seeing lately.
- This kind of underwhelming performance isn't like you.
- Your performance has been substandard lately—how come?
- Isn't it time that you showed us what you're capable of?
- Team members have offered to help you—is that what you want?
- I've had to delegate your tasks to other people—why is that?
- The company is expecting a lot more from you.
- In this company, we take responsibility for our conduct.
- What's gotten into you lately?
- Our department head is looking at your performance closely.
- Taking on more responsibility at work might be a good idea.

HARSH

- We all expect a lot from you, and we're watching.
- You're holding everyone back—this can't go on forever.
- This kind of shoddy performance warrants a verbal warning.
- I've heard people whispering about you; you'd better get it under control.
- I am going to have to write you up immediately.
- You need to earn your pay.
- If you can't pick up the pace, we'll have to let you go.
- If you don't get yourself together by [specific date], you will be terminated.

How to Fire an Employee

PROFESSIONAL

- We can no longer afford to keep you on, unfortunately.
- I'm afraid it's just not working out any longer.
- I'm sorry, but we're going to have to let you go.
- I know you will be much happier elsewhere.
- You're a smart person—we all know you'll land on your feet.
- Someday you will make an excellent employee if you put your mind to it.
- We need to have a serious discussion about your work performance.
- This is going to be your last day with the company.
- We have no choice but to let you go.
- We tried our best to help you but we still didn't get the required work quality.
- Your behavior flies in the face of SOP; we have to let you go.

- I cannot risk losing my job for your mistakes.
- We can't condone what you did; I have no choice but to let you go with cause.
- You broke the rules and now you have to pay the price.
- You leave me no choice but to fire you.
- You know, it's nothing personal—it's just work.
- What do *you* think should happen to you at this point?
- I have a stack of complaints against you; there is nothing left for me to do but fire you.
- You're clearly not a good fit for this company; I have to let you go.
- I'm surprised you made it this far.
- We'll miss your personality, but not your lack of discipline/motivation/dedication.
- It's a shame that our code of conduct allowed you to be here this long.
- I've been more than patient with you.
- Sorry, but you're out.
- It's official—you're fired.
- Firing you has been a long time coming.
- We're going in a different direction, and you won't be along for the ride.
- Feel free to show yourself out.
- Don't let the door hit you on your way out.
- You're probably finished in this business.
- I'm going to enjoy watching you leave.
- You're history.
- You're outta here!

UNPROFESSIONAL

How to Express Urgency

BLATANT

SUBTLE

- Step on it!
- It's go time!
- Let's get a move on it, people!
- We don't have a second to waste.
- Time is of the essence.
- What are you waiting for? Time is a-wasting!
- Failure is not an option, so let's get going!
- Have you heard of the last minute? Well, this is it!
- The clock is ticking, folks.
- Please, let's focus. We only have so much time to finish.
- Please understand the urgency—I need your help now.
- We can get this done if we focus and keep track of time.
- There is no later; there is only now.
- We need to stop wasting time.
- We no longer have the luxury of time to put this off.
- We need to put our wasted time behind us and keep going.
- We need to use what little time we have left.
- Time is a luxury we no longer have.
- Why put off 'til tomorrow what you can do today?
- So much work, so little time.
- This isn't the time to be working on your tan. [sarcastic]

How to Slow Things Down

COURTEOUS

- I think we need to ponder all our options before making a decision.
- A decision this important should be given the time and attention it deserves.
- I appreciate your enthusiasm, but let's slow down for a moment.

- I appreciate your alacrity, but we shouldn't rush this.
- For the sake of thoroughness, I think we should take our time.
- What if we took some time to cogitate on this?
- It might be to our disadvantage to work this quickly.
- We sell no wine before it's time. [joking]
- Can we delay for the purpose of understanding better?
- Let's slow down and really think this through.
- Let's take baby steps while there's still so much time.
- Let's not burn any bridges by moving too quickly.
- It's early yet in the decision-making process.
- There's plenty of time; no need to panic.
- We shouldn't rush into things.
- Everything in good time, my friend.
- Snap decisions rarely work out well in the end.
- Why rush? We've got more than enough time.
- I think that it is a bit premature to make a decision.
- The speed at which we're working is creating a space. for error and confusion.
- Make an error in haste, repent at leisure.
- Only fools rush in.
- Can we slow down a bit? I need to catch my breath!
- We're in no hurry—no need to cause a panic!
- It's madness to move at this speed.
- Haste makes waste.
- One step at a time.
- Your impulsiveness is not serving us well here.
- If I were you, I'd slow down a bit.
- Why run when you can walk?
- No one here is watching the clock, so *slow down*.
- Think, think again, *then* act!
- Let's put the brakes on, okay?
- Whoa, slow down there, speedy!
- Where's the fire?

RUDE

Conflicts and Anger

People who fly into a rage always make a bad landing.
—Will Rogers

Most of your relationships are going to involve conflict from time to time. It is inevitable. Following a few simple principles will help you build powerful synergy and relationships that last, even through the tough times.

1. Communication and compromise

The healthiest relationships involve two basic skills: open communication and compromise. Both of these allow you to effectively handle conflict. The key isn't to always avoid conflicts; rather, it's vital to talk things out openly and stay in control of your emotions—always remembering that the goal is resolution, not victory. If you are always trying to be "one-up" with everyone, you'll never have a satisfying or productive relationship, either at home or at work.

2. Keep on course

One of the most common causes of unresolved conflicts is a discussion that has gone off track or down a dead-end tangent. Stick to the core issue until the conflict is resolved or a compromise is reached. Forget anything that happened more than a month ago, even if you think it is relevant. It will only cause repressed emotions to flare up. Only by ignoring tangential issues that zap your energy, will, and patience will a satisfactory conclusion to the issue at hand be reached.

3. A calm attitude and a clear head

To move past conflict, always approach it with a calm attitude and a clear head. Stay positive, and don't ever resort to the abusive tactics of shouting, name-calling, or blaming. If you are feeling too angry or out of control, take a time-out to calm down. While you're away from the potential source of conflict, visualize the possible positive outcomes that you're working toward and then imagine how your discussion can focus on them. Whatever you do, stay positive during your break and try to avoid seething over the problem.

4. Listen with empathy

One of the most under-appreciated aspects of positive communication during conflict is to simply allow the other person to finish what they are trying to say. Don't interrupt, no matter how much you want to get a word in. Listen attentively and ensure that the other person knows it by keeping comfortable eye contact. When the other person is finished speaking, try to acknowledge and "mirror" their feelings and thoughts before moving on. This helps them feel heard and creates a more empathetic atmosphere. Remember, arguments aren't about winning and losing, but rather compromise and (hopefully) a mutually satisfactory win-win scenario for all concerned.

How to Diffuse a Tense Situation

CONCILIATORY

- It's okay, we just don't see eye to eye on this.
- I'm sorry, I guess we just don't understand each other.
- I think it's generally better to stay away from controversial topics.
- Let's just chalk it up to semantics/Mondays/not getting enough sleep. [joking]
- This topic has caused a lot of trouble for people smarter than we are.
- Neither one of us knows enough to have a productive discussion.
- Well, we should probably stop now before things get too heated.
- There's no reason to fight over little things.
- Don't you feel how problematic this topic is.
- Is it really wise to pursue this discussion?
- Problems such as these tend to create a lot of controversy.
- Let's not allow relatively minor things to put us in a state of conflict.
- I think it's better to stay away from controversial topics.
- This topic has caused a lot of trouble for a lot people.
- It's just a difference of opinion—nothing more, nothing less.
- I think we would all benefit from a less hostile dynamic here.
- Let's take a breather and regroup when we're both calmer.
- Why are we arguing when we actually know so little about this?
- It's not constructive to have so much dissention.
- We shouldn't judge one another—let's be more civil.

AGGRESSIVE

- Aren't we making a big deal out of nothing?
- I don't see respect being offered from either side—let's start over.
- You may want to argue, but I'm not the fighting kind.
- If it's an argument you want, I'm not the person for the job.
- Let's put a stop to this before it gets any worse.
- It wouldn't take much to make this misunderstanding a lot worse.
- All of this bickering isn't getting us anywhere.
- We could wrangle all day, but I'd rather work things out more peacefully.
- We'll continue when everyone is acting less aggressively.
- Would you be less combative when you speak to me, please?
- Why are you getting so excited/upset/irascible?
- Do you think your behavior is bringing us any closer to a resolution?
- Don't jump to conclusions.
- Don't bicker about trivial matters.
- We don't need a war to figure this out.
- Cool your jets.
- Chill out!

How to Stop a Conflict Between Other People

DIPLOMATIC

- It's easy to get upset about this; why, just the other day this happened to me...
- Let's keep this sophisticated, people! [joking]
- I demand a cease fire! [joking]
- Calm down or I'll give you both a pink slip. [joking]
- This discussion could be interesting if everyone was less emotional.

- Before you start arguing, let's go over all the points again.
- Just a moment—I have something to say that might be useful.
- Come on, guys—we need to work as a team here.
- We want to maintain harmony in this environment.
- We are here to collaborate, not bring each other down.
- What if we stopped this discussion and simply let it go for now?
- Let's take a breather and reconvene when everyone's calmer.
- Let's not kill the mood with those topics.
- The project will be in danger if you keep fighting.
- We all need to be cordial with one another.
- You guys need to keep cool before we *all* get into trouble.
- Let's discuss the subject in peace.
- It's pointless to argue at this time.
- We've got better things to do than yell at each other.
- Let's stay constructive, here; arguing is pointless.
- Let's not speak about it any longer, okay?
- You're not getting anything accomplished this way.
- Well, you should probably stop while you're ahead/ before you say something you'll regret.
- That's the kind of behavior we should avoid right now.
- I really dislike this kind of attitude and would like it to stop.
- This is a discussion between equals, not children engaged in a schoolyard fight.
- If you two don't knock it off, I'm going to have to speak with HR/the boss/your father/your mother.
- If you can't settle down, you're both out of here.
- Hey, take a chill pill!
- It looks like the lunatics are in charge of this asylum. [sarcasm]

BLUNT

How to Get Past a Misunderstanding

TACTFUL

- I value our relationship—let's play fair with one another, okay?
- I know this is tough—maybe we can both go over the details once more.
- I believe we can work collaboratively and solve this misunderstanding.
- We're misunderstanding each other and I want to make things better.
- Searching for common ground would help keep us on track, here.
- Two heads think better than one—let's give this another try.
- Solving problems is a part of business/family life/friendship.
- We *both* need to compromise a little to make it work.
- We can rewind to the beginning and start over if you'd like.
- It would help us both to focus on the larger picture.
- Please help me put this problem/issue/conflict to rest.
- I'm sure this makes sense to you—can you explain it to me a bit better?
- I see where you're going with this, but I don't think we're on the same wavelength yet.
- I believe we'll both get further along if we keep our emotions out of it.
- I don't want to clash anymore—let's figure this out once and for all.
- You need to be less hostile so we can solve this problem.
- Once you stop making erroneous assumptions, we'll be able to make real progress.
- Why are you so closed off to the ideas of others?
- C'mon, let's not fight.
- Wow, let it go already!

BLUNT

How to Respond to an Offensive Statement

FRIENDLY

- You certainly have a great command of the idiom! [joking]
- Wow, I can't believe you just said that! [smiling]
- I'm not going to argue with you, but I'm still a bit surprised you said that.
- I'm not sure that many people would agree with you there.
- There are probably some topics that are best avoided, don't you think?
- I don't know whether to take you seriously or not.
- Your statements really upset me—I'm surprised you said that.
- I find that quite disturbing/offensive/tactless/upsetting.
- Is that really what you think?
- Do you realize what you're saying?
- You do know that's completely unreasonable, right?
- Am I hearing you correctly?
- I don't appreciate your choice of words.
- I don't like what you're saying very much.
- What's the point of saying something like that?
- Don't let your words get ahead of your thoughts.
- I think you should rephrase that, don't you?
- I'm not sure you're thinking clearly right now.
- I can't believe you actually said/support/condone that.
- You have to be careful when you make statements like that.
- A statement like that can land you in hot water.
- Did you even hear what you just said?
- Maybe we should talk about the way in which you communicate.
- You should really watch what you say in public.
- If you think like that, there's not much I can do to help you.

CONFRONTATIONAL

- Do you always say everything that pops into your head?
- I distinctly heard what you said and know that you meant it.
- Do you realize you said that out loud?
- Do you take pride in this?
- This is not the right place to talk about this.
- There are things that just shouldn't be said.
- I'm so not in the mood for this.
- You like to upset/shock/unnerve people, don't you?
- If that is your stance, what is there left to talk about?
- If you are happy believing that, I guess I'm happy for you. [sarcasm]
- You should be working as a diplomat with skills like those. [sarcasm]
- I will not tolerate this kind of talk/treatment/attitude!

When Someone Is Angry

GENTLE

- We all have bad days—let's take a second to cool off.
- I'm sure you didn't mean that.
- I know you don't want to offend anybody.
- Let's keep this professional/sophisticated.
- You're taking your point a little too far.
- This isn't the time to let emotions run away from us.
- You're getting a little intense here.
- I feel like you're trying to hurt me—is that the case?
- I find your tone to be a bit provocative/upsetting/confrontational.
- Please don't speak to me that way.
- There is no need to get personal.
- You've reached your boiling point; you need to settle down.
- I'm telling you up front: it's best to avoid that kind of talk.
- Your tone has crossed the line.

CONFRONTATIONAL

- Maybe you should take a walk/get a little fresh air/calm down.
- If you can't control your temper, we'll need to talk some other time.
- Use your inside voice, please.
- I won't tolerate this kind of talk/behavior/tone.
- Are you *trying* to be mean?
- You may have a right to be angry on your own time, but not on mine.
- Your language/tone is offensive and unacceptable.
- Keep a lid on it or you'll be out of here.
- Knock it off!

When Someone Is Insistent/Pressuring You

POLITE

- I'd love to, but I really can't/have to go/don't have the time.
- It's been a pleasure, but I really have to go.
- This simply isn't the right time, unfortunately.
- I would love to help you, but I'm already overcommitted as it is.
- I wish I could be of more help to you, but I can't.
- I must respectfully decline.
- I'm sorry, but I can't help you.
- I don't have time for this at the moment.
- Please leave me alone/stop pushing.
- This conversation is unnecessary.
- Maybe this is the way you get things done, but I don't like it.
- It's useless; you're wasting your efforts on me.
- You'll be wasting your time if you keep talking to me/pushing me.

RUDE

- Why don't you take this up with someone who actually has the time?
- You really should put your energy elsewhere.
- If I need your help, I'll ask for it.
- The answer is no.
- No is a complete sentence.
- You're pushing too hard—stop it!
- Go bother somebody else!

When Someone Is Being Stubborn

PROFESSIONAL

- There is probably more than one way to look at this.
- There are other ways to deal with this issue.
- I can see where you're coming from, but I still must disagree.
- If you thought about this objectively, you would find I'm right.
- I certainly understand how you see it, but I see it differently.
- I'm afraid you didn't understand me very well.
- Are you open to hearing what I have to say?
- If you dig in and say, "I'm right and you're wrong," we won't get anywhere.
- We'll just stay deadlocked forever if neither of us will concede.
- When we both just want to be right, we won't accomplish anything.
- Please listen to reason for a moment.
- You need to be open to others people's perspectives, too.
- The goal of any discussion is to share opinions and be open to the opinions of others.

UNPROFESSIONAL

- If both of us want to come out on top, neither one of us will.
- There's no "I'm always right" in a productive discussion.
- We won't make any progress if you always want the last word.
- You're not always right; I hope you can see that.
- Let's stop acting like children.
- Why is it always your way or the highway?
- If you can't listen to reason, I'm done, here.
- You're just being a blockhead—listen to reason!
- Being pig-headed never helped anyone.
- You must be right since you are so sure. [sarcasm]
- Are you *ever* wrong? [sarcasm]
- You're as stubborn as a mule.

When Someone Is Condescending

POLITE

- I'm sorry to ask you this, but why are you speaking to me like that?
- I'm not sure how to take your comment; would you please explain the intent?
- So that I don't misinterpret your statement, would you please rephrase it?
- Your remarks are hurtful. Would you help me understand where they're coming from?
- Am I hearing you correctly?
- I wonder if I'm misunderstanding what I'm hearing.
- No one likes being talked down to.
- You may not realize how much your remarks hurt.
- Did I just hear you say [repeat the phrase back]?

- Are you trying to insult me or is there something else going on here?
- A little kindness would suit you better.
- I wanted to talk things over with you, but it seems you're not open to that.
- I would appreciate a little more courtesy.
- Not everyone would agree with you, there.
- It's not very nice to talk down to people.
- I'd really like us to figure out a way to work together that doesn't hurt so much.
- That's so condescending—I thought you were a bigger person than that.
- Nobody wins with that attitude.
- Please don't speak to me that way!
- Why do you always make our encounters so difficult?
- Treating people like that will get you nowhere.
- That's no way to act. My opinion is as valuable as yours!
- You're trying to intimidate me/put me down; well, it isn't going to work.
- Do you always give an attitude to those who don't agree with you?
- You don't have to be so contemptible, just because we don't agree.
- Why do you always look down your nose at anyone with a different opinion?
- Who do you think it's okay to insult me like that?
- Can you talk without being quite so rude?
- Don't you have any manners?
- There's really no use talking to you, is there?
- I wish I could be as perfect as you are. [sarcasm]
- Don't cop that "holier than thou" attitude with me.
- Just who do you think you are?
- No wonder you don't have any friends.

RUDE

When Someone Threatens You

TACTIFUL

- Why are you being so hostile?
- That's an unwelcome statement.
- That's crossing a line—I'm sure you'll rethink things.
- There's no reason to act like that—we're professionals, you know.
- Are you trying to upset me?
- Your words are unnecessary and hurtful.
- I would like this to stop.
- This is a waste of time; I'm walking away.
- Are you sure you want to speak to me this way?
- Don't say something you'll regret later.
- Threats are just as harmful as actual violence.
- You don't know what you're saying.
- There is no excuse for incendiary comments like that.
- I don't have time for this.
- I wouldn't provoke me if I were you.
- There's a line of no return in every relationship, and you've just crossed it.
- Your wits have obviously left you.
- You're obviously delusional.
- I won't hesitate to call the authorities if you continue in this vein.
- Threatening me is not something you want to do.
- Are you aware of how much this is going to cost you?
- Do you know what you're risking?
- I don't think you realize the damage you've already caused.
- You can't scare me with mere words.
- If you think I'm frightened, you're mistaken.
- You make me laugh. [sarcasm]

BLUNT

- I won't hesitate to use force if I'm threatened.
- I will counterattack if necessary.
- Come over here and say that again.
- I'm calling the cops.
- Kiss my ass.

When Someone Picks Apart What You Say

COURTEOUS

- Well, I'll just have to disagree with you, there. [joking]
- We all have different opinions; I'm sorry if I misspoke.
- I meant that to be constructive. Please don't take it any other way.
- My words were meant in a professional/kindly manner.
- There are better words than the ones I chose; however, I know you understood me.
- Maybe my words were not the best, but you understand what I am trying to convey.
- Sorry, I didn't think using such precise language was critical just now.
- We're civilized people; what I've said shouldn't make us enemies.
- I was merely stating my opinion.
- I was just saying....
- I didn't expect you to take offense.
- I'm not here to convince anybody.
- I was just making an observation.
- My opinion is just as valid as your opinion.
- I was just making a simple statement.
- I could sugar-coat it, but I don't think that's necessary.
- I think you're taking this too seriously.
- There's no need to work yourself up into a state.
- You shouldn't have such thin skin.

RUDE

- Picking on me isn't going to change anything.
- My words may be imprecise, but I know what I said made sense.
- I could say it differently, but why would I? You get what I'm saying.
- You wouldn't have any reason to pick on me if you made an effort to understand me.
- I'm quite happy to spend all day defending my words, so you'd better get comfortable.
- I just spoke my mind—what's the problem?
- Why can't you accept that we are two people who think differently?
- Why is it so hard to accept that we have differences?
- Stop being so sensitive; there's a big world out there.
- I tend to say what's on my mind—if you don't like it, I can't help you.
- Are there instructions on how one ought to communicate with you? [sarcasm]
- I'm sorry if you were just too stupid to understand my meaning.
- My apologies, Your Majesty! [sarcasm]

When Someone Lies

FRIENDLY

- You're pulling my leg, right? [joking]
- Someone's pants are on fire! [joking]
- Honesty is the best policy. [scolding/joking]
- Honesty is always the best policy, don't you think?
- I really wish I could believe what you're saying.
- People who are straight with me garner my respect.
- I know it's hard, but please be straight with me.
- That's only making a delicate situation worse.
- The truth will set you free.
- It's not fair to mislead people

COMBATIVE

- You and I both know that's not true.
- How about telling me the truth instead?
- Something doesn't add up here.
- Something's rotten in the state of Denmark. [joking]
- How do I know you're lying? Because your lips are moving. [joking]
- What a tangled web we weave, when first we practice to deceive.
- Lying won't get you anywhere.
- You're only making things worse.
- I hate lies—and liars.
- Look me in the eyes and say that again.
- How about being honest for a change? [sarcasm]

When Someone Picks a Fight

CONCILIATORY

- I really don't want this to escalate—I'm sorry if I said the wrong thing.
- If this is going to cause an altercation, I take it all back.
- I certainly didn't mean to offend you.
- I hope what I said won't cause a rift between us.
- I'd prefer to take the high road, here.
- I know you don't really want to pick a fight.
- Let's keep things professional/sophisticated/on the up and up.
- Any relationship we have must be based on respect.
- A true professional puts his/her personal feelings on the back burner.
- There's still time to salvage the situation; it's up to you.
- You don't have to act this way; a reasonable person wouldn't.
- You're a professional—act like one.
- I will not lower myself to your level.

ENGAGED

- Would you please lower your voice/change your tone/ speak more respectfully?
- Think of someone other than yourself!
- Knock it off—I'm not going to engage with you!
- Keep this up and you'll be on the outside looking in.
- Let's stop now if you're going to be immature about it.
- Keep acting like this and you'll be looking for another [job/friend/spouse].
- Are you *looking* for a fight?
- I don't allow anyone to treat me this way.
- If you can't say anything nice, keep your mouth shut.
- Looks like someone is cruising for a bruising.

When Someone Interrupts You

CIVIL

- Please allow me to add just one more thing.
- Sorry, I've got one last point to make.
- Please just let me finish and then you'll have the floor, I promise.
- Please let me continue.
- If I could just go on.
- You're not letting me finish.
- May I finish my thought?
- Won't you allow me to conclude my point?
- If you would just let me get a word in edgewise.
- I wasn't done yet.
- If you'd just listen, all your questions would likely be answered.
- I have a very hard time communicating with you when you keep cutting me off.
- I'd like to finish speaking if that's okay.
- You don't seem to want to hear what I have to say.
- I'm okay listening to you, but are you okay letting me finish?

- I let you speak; now please listen to me for 30 seconds.
- What I say doesn't really matter to you, does it?
- Do you care at all about what I have to say?
- For you to hear me, you'd first have to let me speak.
- Why do you interrupt all the time? Are you afraid of what I have to say?
- For someone who talks so much, you should know how to listen.
- When it's your turn, I'll let you speak.
- Hold your peace until I'm done.
- Don't talk until I'm finished.
- Please let me speak!
- Be quiet and listen to me!
- Shut up already!

BLUNT

When Someone Makes Fun of You

POLITE

- I'm glad you had a laugh at my expense—can we move on? [joking]
- Come on; just admit that you're jealous! [joking]
- I can teach you a thing or two about jokes. [joking]
- Hey, what's so funny?
- Did you know that your humor can be hurtful to some people?
- You're just embarrassing yourself, you know.
- You like laughing at people, don't you?
- I don't appreciate the low blow.
- It's no place for that kind of nonsense.
- I don't like how you're behaving.
- Obviously, humor doesn't come naturally for you.
- Trying to be funny again?
- What makes you think you can say that?
- I don't like the way you're treating me.
- Why do you insist on bringing other people down?

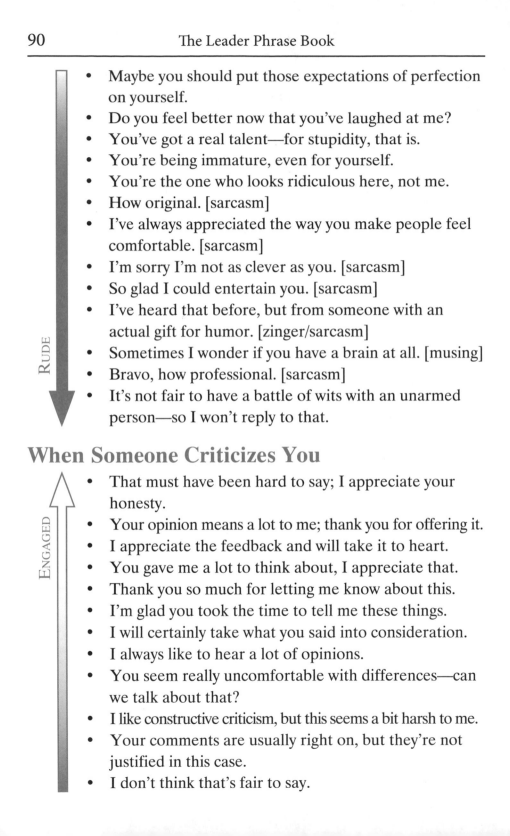

RUDE

- Maybe you should put those expectations of perfection on yourself.
- Do you feel better now that you've laughed at me?
- You've got a real talent—for stupidity, that is.
- You're being immature, even for yourself.
- You're the one who looks ridiculous here, not me.
- How original. [sarcasm]
- I've always appreciated the way you make people feel comfortable. [sarcasm]
- I'm sorry I'm not as clever as you. [sarcasm]
- So glad I could entertain you. [sarcasm]
- I've heard that before, but from someone with an actual gift for humor. [zinger/sarcasm]
- Sometimes I wonder if you have a brain at all. [musing]
- Bravo, how professional. [sarcasm]
- It's not fair to have a battle of wits with an unarmed person—so I won't reply to that.

When Someone Criticizes You

ENGAGED

- That must have been hard to say; I appreciate your honesty.
- Your opinion means a lot to me; thank you for offering it.
- I appreciate the feedback and will take it to heart.
- You gave me a lot to think about, I appreciate that.
- Thank you so much for letting me know about this.
- I'm glad you took the time to tell me these things.
- I will certainly take what you said into consideration.
- I always like to hear a lot of opinions.
- You seem really uncomfortable with differences—can we talk about that?
- I like constructive criticism, but this seems a bit harsh to me.
- Your comments are usually right on, but they're not justified in this case.
- I don't think that's fair to say.

- Is it okay if people do things differently than you?
- This isn't the right place to call someone out like that.
- To each person his or her own flaws.
- When you're pointing a finger at someone, you have four fingers pointing back at you.
- You can't please everyone all of the time.
- Don't you think you're exaggerating, here?
- Do you usually criticize people who are different than you?
- You should take a look at yourself before you start judging others.
- I don't know where all this acrimony is coming from, but please don't direct it at me.
- Doing this only brings you down in the eyes of others.
- People who live in glass houses shouldn't throw stones.
- I won't allow any judgments on that.
- I would never allow myself to comment on that.
- I won't dignify that with a response.
- Don't you ever accept others as they are?
- If I'm not welcome here, just let me know.
- You don't have to stick around if I bother you so much.
- If you have a problem with me, let's just get it out in the open.
- If you're looking for perfection, you shouldn't hang out with me.
- What gives you the right to judge me?
- Who dictates the code of behavior here? You?
- Before you criticize me, take a look in the mirror.
- Do you think *you're* a great example?
- I would acknowledge your comments if I respected you.
- There's only one problem here and it's you!
- Just keep on criticizing me; the entire world knows how perfect *you* are. [sarcasm]
- If I have to be like you to gain your respect, I don't want it.

REJECTING

When Someone Is Defensive

CONCILIATORY

- Please forgive me if I stepped on your toes; I did not mean to upset you.
- I apologize if I hurt your feelings; it was not my intention.
- I didn't mean to offend you; it was only meant in jest.
- Come on, please don't take it like that.
- I was saying it for your benefit/because I care about you.
- Why do I get the feeling that I'm disturbing/upsetting you?
- Why the defensiveness?
- Why are you taking this so hard? It's not as bad as you think.
- Giving *and* accepting advice is part of any relationship.
- Let's discuss this when you feel better/calm down/can see more clearly.
- I don't understand why you're expressing yourself this way.
- There's no need to be so defensive—it's not that big a deal.
- Why are you taking it like that?
- Why do you attribute motives to me that don't exist?
- You shouldn't be so thin-skinned.
- I see that you never let others disagree with you.
- I see that you never let anyone contradict you/speak into your life.
- Why are you so irritable?
- Why do you put up so many walls?
- Why must you always stonewall me?
- You're making a mountain out of a molehill.
- If you were more secure with yourself, you wouldn't be so bummed about this.

OFFENSIVE

- This isn't an attack on you—it's a general statement, so too bad if you took it personally.
- You really need to let this go.
- If only we were all perfect like you. [sarcasm]
- The truth hurts, I'm sure.
- I can't reason with you when you're like this.
- It's impossible to have a conversation with you sometimes.
- There's an 800 number I can recommend if you feel you need help with this.

When Someone Is Doubting You

ASSERTIVE

DEFENSIVE

- You know you can always count on me.
- If there's anyone you can trust here it's me.
- I'm the last person you should be doubting.
- It's my first time in a situation like this.
- You aren't looking at me, are you?
- I've been through this before—have you?
- What do you expect from me?
- Sorry if my past mistakes affected your opinion of me.
- I give *you* the benefit of the doubt.
- I've got that sinking feeling, too.
- I'm sensing the uncertainty, too.
- Listen, it may seem bad now, but it will get better.
- I'm not comfortable with it, either.
- What's the problem? My plan is unimpeachable.
- If you want someone to doubt, look in the mirror.
- Maybe you're the one with the problem.

When Someone Is Avoiding Your Question

COURTEOUS

- And the answer is...? [joking]
- If avoidance were an Olympic event, you'd win the gold medal. [joking]
- It seems like we're having trouble focusing—let me say it another way.
- Okay, I'll put it a different way.
- Let's not dance around the issue any longer.
- Let's get to the heart of the matter.
- Please try your best to answer me.
- I was hoping your answer might be a little more specific.
- Okay, I'll say it again.
- Stop evading me, please.
- Please don't dodge the question.
- You didn't answer my question.
- Do I need to repeat myself?
- Didn't you hear my question?
- Aren't you going to give me an answer?
- Do you need to hear the question again?
- I would like a direct answer to my simple question.
- I'll repeat the question, but only one more time.
- Do you just not know the answer?
- You're dodging the question, aren't you?
- How many times do I have to ask you?
- I didn't realize that I was asking the impossible. [sarcasm]
- Nice way to avoid my question.
- Denial is not just a river in Egypt.
- I demand an answer!

RUDE

When Someone Yells at You

HIGH ROAD

- Speaking calmly will make communicating with me much easier.
- Maybe we need to take a breather, here.
- There is no need to raise your voice.
- Yelling isn't necessary.
- It's very hard for me to communicate with people shouting.
- You could be a little more understanding.
- Try a little tenderness.
- There's no need to raise your voice.
- Yelling isn't necessary.
- What have I done that you would feel the need to speak to me that way?
- More diplomacy and tact would suit you better.
- How about being courteous?
- How about being a little more civil?
- You seem to be getting a little hot under the collar.
- Why the raised voice?
- I think you should go somewhere to calm down.
- Do you need to take a time-out?
- You're going too far.
- Yelling will get you nowhere.
- Breathe for two seconds.
- Why be so hostile?
- Why are you making such an scene?
- You know, it doesn't hurt to be nice.
- I also understand things when they are said softly.
- You're crossing a line, here.
- Seriously, you should calm down.

LOW ROAD

- Show a little class.
- Why make such a scene?
- Are you aware that you're screaming?
- Talking that loudly doesn't make you any smarter or more convincing.
- What is this supposed to accomplish?
- Is that it? Are you done yelling now?
- I'm surprised by even that much tact out of you. [sarcasm]
- What eloquence. [sarcasm]
- Keep talking that loudly and you'll be talking to an empty room.
- I refuse to let anyone speak to me like that.
- I've heard enough—bye!
- I'm not deaf!

When Someone Swears at You

SUBTLE

- Whoa, easy with the language! [joking]
- My virgin ears! [joking]
- You're better than that.
- A little diplomacy can go a long way.
- There are other ways to say that.
- This kind of behavior doesn't suit you well.
- It's not really nice to say that.
- That kind of talk is unnecessary.
- You've disappointed me.
- I'm not feeling comfortable with you right now.
- We can come back to this when you calm down.
- Losing control never solves anything.
- Is it really necessary to say that?
- How about being nice?
- How about being a little civil?
- Well, that's offensive!
- Watch your language, please.

AGGRESSIVE

- In case you were not aware, we speak politely around here.
- If you can't say something nice, don't say anything at all.
- You're belying your education/upbringing when you talk like that.
- I don't understand how you can take pleasure in being rude.
- It must be exhausting to carry around so much anger inside.
- Why are you being so offensive?
- Can't you speak without being vulgar?
- Do you ever think before speaking?
- What does it gain you to be nasty like that?
- Keep speaking like that and you'll be talking to yourself.
- I'm overwhelmed by your abundant tact. [sarcasm]
- Congratulations, how intelligent. [sarcasm]
- Knock it off!

When Someone Changes the Topic

POLITE

- Good point—we'll get back to that in a second.
- Let's get back to what we were talking about.
- Let's get back to the subject at hand.
- I feel that we're slightly off topic now
- Let's stick to the agenda before moving on to new topics.
- I think we were still talking about [topic at hand], no?
- There's no use moving on until we're finished with the subject at hand.
- I think we're veering too far afield from the issue at hand.
- It seems to me that we weren't speaking about that.
- You seem to be deflecting the main issue.
- It seems like you're trying to muddy the waters.

RUDE

- Is this topic really along the same lines?
- That has nothing to do with the current conversation.
- You're approaching this conversation as though it were a monologue.
- I don't think we've resolved the issue yet, do you?
- Talking to you is like being in a revolving door.
- I think you're just trying to confuse the issue.
- Please don't change the subject.
- Don't try to divert the conversation.
- I feel like I'm talking to a brick wall.
- I wasn't done yet!

When Someone Insults You

CIVIL

- You seem a little anxious/overworked/upset—what can I do to help?
- Whoa, let's keep this sophisticated! [joking]
- I like the polite version of you much better!
- Aw, that wasn't very nice.
- I think you're exaggerating a bit, here—don't you?
- I really don't want to argue with you.
- Please be more careful with your choice of words.
- This isn't the right place to call someone out like that.
- What did I ever do to you to warrant that?
- Why are you being so rude?
- Is it really necessary to say that?
- I can't do much when someone is speaking to me like that.
- I always treated you with respect. What's the problem?
- There are some things that just shouldn't be uttered.
- I never allow anybody to talk to me this way.
- This is going too far.

- I don't have to stick around for this.
- I don't want to hear you talk like this ever again.
- Keep on crossing the line and I'll [...]!
- If you're tired, go to take a nap.
- Just tone it down, okay?
- Knock it off!
- Bravo, what diplomacy. [sarcasm]
- Have fun insulting me; obviously we're all here for that. [sarcasm]

When Someone Is Violent

- Violence is never the answer.
- I thought you had more respect for me.
- This behavior will not benefit anybody.
- I don't appreciate you hitting me.
- Please don't put your hands on me.
- Keep your hands to yourself, please.
- You've definitely crossed the line of respect
- I think you really need help.
- Clearly you have a problem.
- You need to relax.
- You can lose your job for this.
- This is the last time you'll ever do that.
- What you did can put you in jail.
- Stop this right now.
- I will not tolerate that again.
- Hey, you've crossed the line!
- Get a hold of yourself.
- You need to be in a mental institution/behind bars.
- I'm tempted to knock you into yesterday.
- Are you happy now? [sarcasm]
- Do you treat everybody like this?
- If you come at me again, I will retaliate, I promise.

THREATENING

- Touch me again and I'm calling the police/authorities/ HR.
- That was quite possibly the worst mistake you've ever made in your life.
- Do that again and I'll ruin your life.
- I'm calling the cops.
- You're finished here.
- Care to see my black belt?

Diplomacy

Diplomacy is the art of letting someone have your way.
—Daniele Vare

Diplomats are people who have very specialized skills and who are tasked with an incredibly difficult mission. The forum for their activities is often quite public, so "working under the radar" is not always possible. If you need to engage in diplomatic tactics as part of your job, here are a few tips that will prove useful.

1. Engage the trust of the other side

Imagine that you are a consul or an ambassador working to represent the interests of the U.S. government. During complex meetings and functions, you are in charge of discussing and resolving very delicate situations that have a great deal riding on them, all while maintaining friendly relations, if possible. If you are able to speak like a leader—someone who exudes confidence, respectfulness, authority, and above all, honesty—you will be trusted with critical information in turn.

2. Practice communication

Polish your communication skills the way you tone your muscles at the gym. Attend speaking courses and communication classes, watch documentaries and interviews, and listen to podcasts from elites in their field. Make note of any interesting, compelling, or unusually persuasive language you learn and then use it to your advantage in your own communications.

3. Embrace the art of doubletalk

It is important for a diplomat to know when to tell the truth, the whole truth, and nothing but the truth, and when to tell only the portion of the truth that is required by the situation at hand. As Carey McWilliams once said, "In order to be a diplomat one must speak a number of languages, including double-talk." Or, as Emily Dickenson once wrote, "Tell the truth but tell it slant."

4. Appear strong under pressure— even if you aren't

Winston Churchill displayed an amazing ability to adapt under conditions of great stress and pressure. He did so by mastering the language of a leader and by peppering his diplomacy with humor. When he was facing the tyranny of Adolph Hitler, Churchill said, "An appeaser is one who feeds a crocodile, hoping it will eat him last." You can see that Churchill had absolute command of the idiom and could deploy it with great effect. By following his example, you'll find that people will more quickly gravitate to your point of view, which is exactly what you hope to accomplish in any negotiation. (See Part 5 for more on actual negotiation tactics.)

How to Open Up a Topic for Debate

FRIENDLY ↑

- I love a lively debate! Let's talk about [topic].
- There's no time like the present to discuss this.
- I'd love to have your take on this.
- Let's open this up for debate, shall we?
- Please speak freely—I think we'll work better that way.
- I'd like for us to bat around some ideas for a moment.
- I've wanted to talk with you about this for a long time.
- Only by talking things through can we help one another succeed.
- I want to listen and I want to understand.
- I'd like for us to elaborate a bit on [topic].
- The topic is now open for discussion.
- I know our discussions will end up being constructive.
- Our discussions have always led us toward an amicable solution.
- I'm not looking to simply talk; I'm looking to make something happen.
- The topic for this session is [topic].
- I suggest we all share our views about [topic].
- Let's dive into the subject of [topic].
- I'm hoping we can come to an understanding about [topic].
- Whatever results from our discussions will be just fine.
- Real discourse can only help us during tough times.
- A good rivalry will only make us both stronger.
- Anything we discuss must lead to positive results.
- Dialogue is absolutely necessary.
- We should all be able to express ourselves without fear.

CONFRONTATIONAL

- I want to eliminate all ambiguities and remove all objections.
- Let's each go over our side of the argument.
- We'll all feel better if we eliminate the complexities right from the start.
- Any discussion we have needs to lead to something concrete.
- Let's begin this by first recognizing the problem(s) we face.
- I hope nothing negative will come from our discussions.
- I have a hard time getting past our differences—how can we fix that?
- I'm okay with an open discussion—are you?
- Let's hash this out right now.
- Well, we have to hammer this out sooner or later, so it might as well be now.
- Let's just get this out in the open, shall we?

How to Wrap Up a Debate

FRIENDLY

- I am so glad we talked!
- I feel really good about today's conversation.
- I vote that we wrap up the proceedings and go out for a beer.
- I can't take in any more information—my brain is fried! [joking]
- It's okay that we don't see eye to eye—in fact, it keeps things interesting.
- The danger of continuing our little talk is that I might never want it to end.
- I believe everything has been resolved—any final words?
- Seems like we're back on track; I say we end things here.
- Maybe we can revisit this at a later date—what say you?

DIRECTIVE

- I could listen to you for hours, but I just don't have the time.
- I learned a lot talking to you, but I have another engagement.
- I'd like to continue with this, but I'm late for [task].
- This conversation will take more time than I have right now.
- Let it read in the minutes that we closed the debate at [time].
- Thank you, but this subject is now closed.
- There's really no reason to continue, is there?
- It's not an argument that has an easy solution.
- For now, we'll have to agree to disagree.
- Sorry, I can no longer bring anything helpful to this debate.
- People smarter than we are don't agree on this—let's just drop it.
- I know the usual outcome of this kind of exchange, so I'd rather avoid it.
- If we continue in this vein, the conversation will end badly.
- My conviction that we should continue this discussion is rapidly diminishing.
- To close these talks would be a blessing to everyone involved, I think.
- There's really no point in continuing.
- Let's terminate the proceedings.
- I will not continue with this for another minute.
- I think we've crossed a line, here.
- This is a dead-end subject.
- That's it, I'm walking out.
- This conversation is over.
- I'm outta here!

How to Open a Public Speech

FORMAL

- Ladies, gentlemen, and honored guests...
- My dear brothers and sisters...
- With solemnity in my voice...
- With the greatest humility...
- Thank you for coming, all of you.
- I am filled with gratitude to be speaking with you today.
- It is not by happenstance that we are all together today.
- On behalf of [honored guest or entity], I'd like to begin by saying...
- This is an auspicious occasion for everyone involved.
- I would like to start by saying...
- I will begin by offering a simple [acknowledgment/ homage] to [honored person's name].
- I stand here before all of you with an open mind and an honest heart.
- There's a time when one ought to use precisely the right words, and that time is now.
- This is a proud day for [honored guest or entity].
- Let me begin with a simple thought.
- Before I begin, I would like to say that I am very happy to see all of you here today.
- I've got a few points to make here today, so please bear with me.
- Now that I've got you all cornered [joking], I'd like to start by saying...
- Hello, all! I will start by introducing myself.
- I promise this'll be short and sweet!
- Ladies and germs...

CASUAL

How to Close a Speech

FORMAL ↑

- I am filled with gratitude that I was able to speak with you today.
- It has been an honor speaking with you today.
- Thank you for allowing me to speak to you today.
- I will end by acknowledging our mutual commitment to [company/project/cause].
- In closing, allow me to reiterate one last time...
- Allow me to close by recapping my major points.
- I will close by saying...
- As Theodore Roosevelt said, "Keep your eyes on the stars but keep your feet on the ground."
- I expect a fair number of questions, so let me turn the podium over to you.
- I appreciate your attention; I hope you all have a great day/night.
- The best way to end is with a few questions—ones that I hope I have answers to. [joking]
- And now for the Q & A.
- All good things must come to an end. [joking]
- So I guess this is the way this speech ends—not with a bang, but with a whimper. [joking]
- Thank you, you've been great!

CASUAL ↓

How to Accuse Someone of Something

TACTFUL ↑

- I truly don't mean to offend you, but something has come to my attention.
- An unfortunate situation has come up that I need to talk to you about.
- It's really hard for me to say this, but...
- If I didn't care about you, I wouldn't say this...
- It's not my place to point fingers, but...

BLUNT

- I regret that I have to be so direct, but...
- It's difficult for me to accuse you of anything, but...
- I would be remiss if I didn't bring this to your attention.
- There's something I need to confront you about.
- You need to take responsibility for your conduct.
- With all due respect, I know you did this.
- There's no smoke without fire.
- It's time you faced the music.
- Will you never admit to your wrongs?
- Don't you feel guilty?
- I blame you.
- You're at fault here—just admit it.
- I'm calling you out.
- It's all your fault.
- 'Fess up!
- If it walks like a duck...

How to Call for a Consensus

CIVIL

- I think we can work something out if we all worked together.
- Compromise can form a bridge between our differences.
- With solidarity, we can conquer any problem.
- The question is a tough one; all the better to form a consensus.
- We'll succeed if we find common ground.
- I am positive we can come to an accord.
- I know that we can come to a compromise.
- It's time that we all came together and made this happen.
- It's vital that we forge a consensus.

- I think we'd all agree that we need a unified solution.
- This issue is complex, but good things will happen if we come to a consensus.
- Collaboration is the only way forward at this time.
- At the end of the day our needs are all the same.
- My options are completely open—are yours?
- It's time to make some concessions.
- Let's seek an accord right now.
- There's no need for complete capitulation on either side.
- We need to get on the same page before coming to an agreement.
- Try to see it another way so that we can come to an agreement.
- To solve this problem, everyone involved needs to be willing to give in a little.
- Why can't we all get on the same page?
- If no agreement comes out of this, nobody benefits.
- Either we come to an accord, or we have a serious problem.
- Nobody wins if everyone loses.

FORCEFUL

How to Address a Difference of Opinion

ACCEPTING

- If we all agreed on everything, what would be the point of talking? [joking]
- We obviously have a difference of opinion, and that's okay.
- I certainly understand why you would think that—tell me more.
- You seem to know a lot about this—but how can you be so sure?
- There's probably room for some interpretation/nuance here.

- I'm sure we will come to an agreement in time.
- Just because we don't agree on everything doesn't mean that we can't agree on *something*.
- Both of us clearly have misgivings, but let's try to move forward.
- I understand how you see it; I just see it differently.
- We're not speaking the same language yet—let's try harder.
- Do you think we could meet somewhere in the middle on this?
- In your opinion, how can we best reach common ground?
- Let's not get bogged down by a small difference of opinion.
- What do we need to do to come to an agreement?
- If I may react/respond to that.
- I would like to argue that...
- Do you at least agree that...?
- I know many people who would think differently.
- This subject has been debated for hundreds of years.
- Not all opinions are equal.
- There's clearly a difference of opinion, here.
- No-one's opinion is priviledged.
- That's not my understanding of the issue.
- You might want to reconsider your opinion on this.
- As you know, I have a hard time subscribing to that point of view.
- The truth of any situation is relative.
- Try to realize what you're saying here.
- Don't you think you're overstating the issue a bit?

REJECTING

- I don't see how you can rationalize/justify your comments/beliefs.
- It's obvious we don't see eye to eye.
- There's no point in discussing this any further since we don't agree.
- We're nowhere even close to an agreement, so we should just call it a night.
- If we can't come to an agreement, there's no point in continuing our dialog.
- Don't speak about what you don't know.
- I'm not in the mood to tolerate such nonsense.
- Your convictions are heretical.
- Come back down to planet Earth!

How to Avoid a Sensitive Topic

CONCILIATORY

- Maybe it's best to leave that alone for now.
- Let's change subject and remain blissful. [joking]
- Believe me, this topic is nothing but trouble. [joking]
- You know what they say about Pandora's Box. [joking]
- I'd rather be boiled alive than talk about that. [joking]
- This has become kind of a sensitive subject, you know?
- Let's not open a can of worms.
- Let's stick to the matter at hand, shall we?
- Let's keep this positive vibe going and not talk about that.
- Can we consider discussing something else?
- Maybe we shouldn't touch on that topic just now.
- Let's table this discussion for another time.
- I'd rather not talk about that, if that's okay with you.
- It probably would be unprofessional to proceed along those lines.
- If we don't change the subject, I can see trouble brewing.

- We've talked this through already so let's not go there again.
- I hate confrontation, so let's just avoid that whole topic, okay?
- This is getting a little uncomfortable. Can we let it slide for a little while?
- This is never a good topic of conversation—for anyone.
- Can we move away from this topic—at least until I leave?
- I've heard this tune before, and it gets more discordant every time.
- The last time we discussed that, it took a [week/fortnight/month of Sundays] to calm everyone down.
- That topic is taboo around here.
- We don't have much time, so let's just keep it light.
- Do you think this discussion will bring us any closer?
- Pursuing this dialog any further is pointless.
- Don't you realize how much of a problem this topic is for me?
- That topic is five miles of bad road. Let's pick something more productive.
- Things only get more tense with that kind of talk.
- Ruminating on this will only lead to heartache, or worse.
- It's conversational suicide to even consider a topic like that.
- Oh boy, here we go again.
- I don't want to talk about it, end of story.
- I will not engage with you about this.

BLUNT

How to Advise/Make Suggestions

GENTLE

- I have some thoughts but I want to tread lightly.
- There is wisdom in the counsel of many—would you like to hear my thoughts?
- We're pretty good friends, right? What would you think of [suggestion]?
- I have some ideas—would you like to hear them?
- We've gotten to know each other so well, I think we can get personal.
- I'm just thinking out loud, but what if you...?
- This is only my opinion, but...
- May I be honest with you?
- May I speak frankly?
- Do you mind if I offer you a suggestion?
- Don't take this the wrong way, but...
- It might be a good idea if you...
- I'm not trying to make you feel badly, but...
- I don't mean any disrespect, but...
- I hope my suggestion doesn't come across the wrong way.
- I hope you don't find this offensive, but perhaps you should consider [suggestion].
- You don't have to take it, but here's some good advice.
- I would recommend that you...
- Let me give you some valuable advice about this.
- The best thing for you to do at this point would be to...

DIRECTIVE

- This might help you out.
- Let me just say this...
- A word of advice...
- Seems like you could use an objective opinion.
- You could not be more wrong—you need to listen to reason.
- It's your funeral.

How to Respond to Unwanted Advice/Suggestions

POLITE

- Thank you for caring enough to speak into my life.
- It's very kind of you and I really appreciate your honesty.
- Wow, I never saw it that way. Thanks!
- I will certainly take that into consideration.
- You gave me a lot to think about, thank you.
- I'm really pleased you took the time to tell me these things.
- Thank you so much for letting me know about this.
- If you have any other suggestions, please let me know.
- Thanks for pointing that out.
- That's good to know.
- I always like to hear others' opinions.
- I'm open to whatever you might suggest.
- Thanks, I appreciate your concern.
- Thanks for wanting to help.
- It's very nice for you to worry about me, but you really shouldn't.

- You're very kind to try to help me, but I'm happy like this.
- I get what you're saying, but I think I'm okay with my plan.
- I know you mean well, but I prefer to keep my own counsel on the matter.
- What experience/knowledge do you base your advice on?
- Thanks for your concern, but I'm doing just fine.
- I will decide to take my own action on the matter.
- I'm fully aware of what I'm doing, thanks. [sarcasm]
- I don't need anyone to look out for my interests but myself.
- Your advice is worth about what I paid for it.
- If I wanted your opinion/advice, I would have asked for it.

CONFRONTATIONAL

When Someone Accuses You of Something

POLITE

- Ah, court is in session! [joking]
- I'm not sure how you arrived at that conclusion, but I want to hear you out.
- Please let me help you find out what *really* happened.
- I'm hurt that you would even think that—what can I do to convince you otherwise?
- I wish I could say I did it, but that would be a lie.
- I understand why you would think that, but it's simply not the case.
- I'm afraid I'm not following you at all.
- You can't be any further from the truth.
- The burden of proof is on the accuser.
- I'm going to have to defend myself, here.

CONFRONTATIONAL

- It's very easy to assume when we don't know.
- I have *no* idea what you're talking about.
- Don't blame me—it wasn't my responsibility.
- You're speaking completely out of context.
- I will not allow you to say things that are inaccurate.
- If you knew the facts, you'd see that it's not my fault.
- You should be sure before you start accusing others.
- I don't think we're getting to the heart of the issue.
- I have other things to do than answering to polemics.
- Before you point a finger at someone, you should give him/her a chance to speak.
- The problem is much more complex than that.
- Pointing fingers doesn't help anything.
- I will neither confirm nor deny that.
- Let he who is without sin cast the first stone.
- People who live in glass houses shouldn't throw stones.
- Clearly something went terribly wrong, but it wasn't my fault.
- Please understand this was never my intention.
- It's nobody's fault, so it's useless to assign blame.
- Seems that I'm a victim of circumstance.
- How did you come to this erroneous conclusion?
- I'd like to know who or what is your source?
- Whatever happened to "innocent until proven guilty"?
- This didn't happen on my watch!
- *Mea culpa.* [sarcasm]
- I will sue you for slander/libel.

When You Are the Subject of Rumors

POLITE

CONFRONTATIONAL

- I'm sorry, but I never comment on half-truths and innuendoes.
- I only *wish* my life were that interesting! [joking]
- This is an ongoing investigation/problem, so unfortunately I can't comment on it.
- I don't have any further information and will not release any statements at this time.
- There are more important things going on in the world than this.
- That is a misinterpretation of what I actually said/did.
- My advice on these rumors is to let them go.
- Rumor and innuendo, that's all it is
- Rumors are not the best sources of facts.
- This is just rampant insinuation and I have nothing to say.
- I'm not going to discuss that.
- It would be unwise for me to respond to such nonsense.
- Let's not perpetuate such infantile behavior by giving it lip service.
- I didn't want to give this gossip any attention, but I must say something...
- Such gossip will not be tolerated much longer.
- These are half-baked lies that don't dignify a response.
- I don't report to you and will not respond.
- Since when am I accountable to you?
- So what?

Negotiation

Negotiating means getting the best of your opponent.
—Marvin Gaye

Knowing how to negotiate is one of the most important skills of a good leader. It pays to be good at it, and it isn't as difficult as it seems on the surface. Far from being the sole provenance of salespeople and buyers, anyone who needs to interact with other people will inevitably need to negotiate. A young married couple negotiates on how to share a living space. Teachers negotiate with children as a part of working with their class. Bankers almost never get what they want without working their deal. And musicians must negotiate a fair price for the fruits of their labor. If you don't know how to negotiate or are too afraid to, you risk becoming marginalized. Here are some tips to help you become a better negotiator (note that there is by necessity some overlap here with the section on diplomacy).

1. Gain the trust of others

Leaders who know how to negotiate well are able to quickly gain the trust of the parties involved. Part of gaining trust is having a certain amount of transparency—but not too much!—regarding your desires and goals. When people know what you want, they will be more likely to trust you.

2. Don't justify yourself

This is the downside and converse of the first point: the more you expose your thoughts and goals, the more you open yourself up to disapproval, criticism, and rejection. Sometimes being more inscrutable will work to your advantage. During negotiations, keep your cards close to your chest if it's something that could weaken your position. Likewise, when laying out your intentions, be succinct—say only what you need to and then stop talking. Leave a space for silence. By justifying your goals you may come across as underwhelming or indecisive or, worse yet, defensive.

3. Don't let them see you sweat

Poor or inexperienced negotiators allow their opponents to see their weakness. You never want to cede your advantage like this. Keep a poker face and project nerves of steel, even if you are quaking inside. Practice this with smaller deals and then work your way up to bigger ones.

4. Be willing to walk away

The person who is least invested in the outcome—or who *appears* to be the least invested—has the most power. You're in charge. You set the agenda, which includes when you will walk away.

5. Silence is golden

You do not always have to do all the talking. Sometimes a period of silence or even a break in negotiations can do more in less time than trying to ramrod a solution down the other side's throat. Silence also creates a space for discomfort and awkwardness, which unsettles your opponent and may make them more willing to concede.

How to Ask a Question

FORMAL

- Would you be so kind as to answer this one question?
- I do have one question, if you don't mind.
- I'd like to raise an important point, if I may.
- I apologise if we've covered this before, but....
- I am seeking to understand this matter more fully.
- While it may sound rhetorical, my question is...
- Another question remains to be clarified...
- I'd like to hear your solution to this.
- Here's a simple question.
- I'll go the direct route and simply ask this question.
- I have something to ask.
- You probably know the answer to this.
- Here's something I've been wondering about.
- I was wondering if...
- Anyone know the answer to this?

CASUAL

- I'm stumped—can someone help me out here?
- Inquiring minds want to know.

How to Stall

PROFESSIONAL

- That's a very good question—allow me to think before I respond.
- What an interesting idea/thought/question.
- Please allow me a moment to ponder the ramifications before I speak.
- I will need to gather my thoughts here for a moment.
- That's going to require more research.
- I need to gather all the facts before I weigh in.
- That's on a lot of peoples' minds these days.
- I am really glad you brought that up.
- You always make such excellent points.

CASUAL

- Your inquiry is a legitimate one and calls for a qualified response.
- I think you are raising a very interesting point.
- That's a good question and it deserves a clear answer.
- I'll give you the short answer; we can talk more in-depth later on.
- Let me think about it, as times/the facts have changed.
- That takes a good deal of specialized knowledge.
- Let me think on it for a second.
- I don't recall hearing that before.
- Can you clarify or restate the question/your point?
- I'm not sure I understand where you're going with that.
- Why do you ask?
- Who knows?
- I honestly don't even know what to say.

How to Emphasize a Point

POLITE

- Allow me to stress just how important this is.
- I would like to emphasize this point, if I may.
- I cannot stress enough just how critical this is.
- Precision of language is of utmost importance, here.
- Please take especial note of this point.
- I really want to emphasize the fact that...
- And you can quote me on this...
- What I have to say next is very important.
- While there are many opinions on this, here is my take.
- Here's the bottom line.
- Let me be clear about this.
- Let me pick my words very carefully, here.
- Let me make this point even more clear.
- Here is where the rubber meets the road.

ABRUPT

- There are no ifs, ands, or buts about this.
- It really just comes down to this...
- The fact that is most relevant/important is....
- An important thing to realize is...
- I can say unequivocally that...
- Let me put it another way.
- I think that it is important to understand that...
- As God is my witness....
- I'll take it one step further.
- I'm not going to beat around the bush, here.
- I've said it before and I'll say it again...
- You might want to sit up and take note of this.
- Now pay attention!

How to Convince

COURTEOUS

- What can I do or say to persuade you?
- Please allow me to plead my case.
- There's a lot of research that supports this; for example...
- Anyone who knows about this will say that...
- Time and experience have shown me that...
- Experts would agree that...
- Give me a few minutes and I promise you, you'll change your mind.
- I'd like to encourage you to look at the other side for a moment.
- Given enough time, I know that I can win you over.
- The best in the field will agree with me that...
- I believe I can sway you if you'll just listen to the facts.
- Your logic must be able to discern the veracity of what I'm saying.

- All I ask is that you revisit the issue.
- The truth will set you free.
- I have no right to hijack your conscience, but...
- You're smart enough to know the truth when you see it.
- Am I not swaying your opinion?
- If you opened your eyes to the facts, I think you would understand.
- It's as plain as the nose on your face.
- How can you *not* see my point?
- Anyone with an ounce of common sense would know that.
- Don't be so obdurate and just listen for a moment!

RUDE

How to Accept a Proposal

- I am gratified to say that I accept without reservations.
- I accept, with honor and humility.
- I can't tell you what an honor this is for me.
- This is a proud moment for both of us.
- I'm touched to know that you made me a part of this.
- I'm on board with that.
- I hear you and agree.
- I'm with you all the way.
- There's nothing I would rather do.
- Let's make it happen.
- Let's shake hands on it.
- Let's pull the trigger on this.
- Sign me up on the dotted line.
- That's a no-brainer.
- My answer is a big yes.
- Count me in.
- Fine by me!

FORMAL

CASUAL

How to Reject a Proposal

POLITE

- I must respectfully decline at this time.
- I'm sorry to have to say no to the generous proposition you've made.
- I apologize that I am unable to accept your offer right now.
- Unfortunately I cannot accept your excellent proposal at this time.
- I appreciate your suggestion, but we must find another way.
- I must decline with humility.
- I have already accepted a similar proposal, so I must say no.
- While I would love to say yes, I don't believe I could get it past my [boss/spouse/parents].
- I don't think it would be wise for us to go forward at this time.
- This could have worked out under better circumstances.
- The decision is out of my control, sorry.
- I don't think your plan is the right one for this situation.
- I can't work with you on that, sorry.
- Not at this time; thanks, though.
- We just can't afford the risk/expenditure/complication right now.
- Your tenaciousness is impressive, but I just can't move on this.
- Your solution is risky; I just can't run with it.
- Your idea raises more questions than it answers.
- It's a no-go.
- It's simply out of the question.

BLUNT

- I don't think it's going to work.
- I'm going to have to put the kibosh on this.
- Only if you pay me for it! [joking]
- No can do.
- That's not gonna work for me.
- Maybe when pigs fly! [joking]

How to Sell Something to Someone

PUSH-THROUGH

- If you don't move on this now you'll regret it.
- You'd better buy now before you miss out.
- Don't let this be the one that got away.
- Get it now before it's gone.
- Take it home today—you won't regret it.
- This is a one day sale; by tomorrow it will be gone.
- Tomorrow you'll be a day late and a dollar short.
- This is the deal of the century.
- This special price is only good until [date].
- There won't be another sale like this until [date].
- There's a lot of interest in this, so you'd better move on it.
- This is your lucky day!
- The deal is almost irresistible.
- You're buying quality.
- It won't stay at that price for very long.
- I have one and it changed my life.
- You deserve it
- You're worth it.
- You'll be the envy of your peers/colleagues/friends.
- What would it take for you to decide today?
- It's the crème de la crème.
- This is a great value/bargain.
- Quality and price—you can't ask for more.

LOW PRESSURE

- Please consider it—you'll be glad you did.
- I think you'll be happy with it.
- What have you got to lose?
- It's only money, after all.
- What's the worst that could happen?
- You can always return it.
- Nothing ventured, nothing gained.
- Only you can make that decision.

How to Bargain

POSITIVE

- I'm sure we can get to a win-win, here.
- I know we can work something out.
- That sounds better—let's talk some more.
- Let's make a deal.
- Let's each go halfway and we'll be done.
- I saw a lower/higher price on that just the other day.
- Meet me in the middle; it's the only answer.
- We both want this deal to work out, so let's make it happen.
- Can't you budge a bit more on the price? After all, I've made concessions, too.
- We both want a successful outcome here, right?
- I have no problem walking away from this.
- The clock is ticking.
- You'll have to do better than that.
- Help me out, here.
- I expected a better offer from you.
- It's not personal, it's business.
- We're both trying to make a living, here.

NEGATIVE

- Your competitor is going to be happy about this.
- Do you think your rigidity is serving you?
- I'll have to walk if we can't come to terms.
- I'm not made of money.
- Wow, that's insulting.
- [silence]

When You Are in a Stalemate

POSITIVE

- I know you want this as much as I do—what can you do for me?
- I feel that we are one step away from shaking hands.
- Here are my concessions—what are you willing to bend on?
- I've given a bit, now it's your turn.
- How will we proceed with this two-sided quandary?
- It seems we're at a standoff—do you have any ideas?
- We're in a deadlock. What should we do?
- I don't know how we're going to get out of this.
- Can't we just agree on something?
- Both sides are in a stalemate—what do you suggest?
- Do you see a way out of this?
- Unfortunately, we've reached a dead-end and nobody is budging.
- I can't stand this constant back and forth, and I know you can't, either.

NEGATIVE

- I wish we could get out of this quagmire.
- I'm not sure where we should go from here.
- Maybe I should just take my business elsewhere.
- You're not the only game in town.
- This has been a waste of my time and yours.

How to Call for Compromise

CIVIL

- With our mutual respect, I'm sure we'll come to a decision that suits us both.
- I know we can reach an agreement if we work together.
- We both want what's best—how can we make that happen?
- Compromise is always the way to go.
- Aren't we all looking for a win-win, here?
- If you agree, let's shake hands on it.
- Let's move forward in the spirit of compromise.
- Coming to an agreement is the best thing for all concerned.
- I think we both need to accommodate each other, here.
- I'd really like to come to an understanding about this issue.
- You won't regret coming to a decision that benefits all parties.
- I think we've achieved a lot through our negotiations, but it's decision time.
- I'm willing to listen to you if you listen to me.
- Let's both make an effort.
- I think we should agree to settle and move on.
- I hope you're willing to at least consider my parameters.
- There's no magic solution; it's all give-and-take.
- Meet me in the middle—it's the only answer.
- We'll be fine if I give a little and you give a little.
- Let's each go halfway and we'll be done.

BOLD

- I can't imagine us *not* coming to an agreement.
- I can't go back to my [boss/family/colleagues] without settling this.
- There is no perfect solution, so let's just get it over with and settle.
- I'm willing to engage in some give-and-take—are you?
- At least meet me halfway.
- I guess we'll get to that place when you're finally willing to compromise.
- Let's get this done once and for all.
- Let's just flip a coin. It's better than going on and on about it forever.
- Come on, work with me on this.
- Let's cut to the chase and quit wasting everyone's time.

Problem Solving

Leaders are problem solvers by talent and temperament, and by choice.
—Harlan Cleveland

Great leaders are great problem solvers. Being able to put solutions into action puts you at center stage and provides people with the direction they often need. Applying the following tips will help you attack and solve any issue with aplomb:

1. Diagnose

Ask an unlimited number of questions to first find out what the problem actually is—no sense in coming up with a great solution for the wrong problem! Think of a doctor who asks multiple searching questions while performing an examination. This gives her a great deal of information that will be invaluable in coming up with a diagnosis. And don't be afraid to ask "dumb" questions—give yourself permission to explore every possibility.

2. Advocate

Once you understand what you're up against you have to help people realize the magnitude of the problem and the potential pitfalls of not solving it effectively. This involves discussing the full scope of the issue, including any downstream effects, and persuading them that they need to be part of the solution.

3. Strategize

If you fail to plan, you may as well plan to fail. Outline a step-by-step plan as to how the problem will be tackled. Rather than merely giving commands, find a way to make people believe that the solution is their own idea. If you are facing opposition, help people recognize how your solution will benefit them personally.

4. Delegate and follow up

Be sure the group has a handle on the problem and can effectively put your plans into action. Don't be afraid to delegate, but be sure you check in regularly to see how things are progressing.

How to Address/Acknowledge a Problem

URGENT

- We need to find a way out of this immediately, if not sooner.
- We have a problem on our hands that must be solved, *now*.
- We've got to figure this out *right now*.
- We need to find an answer to this asap.
- We must get to the bottom of this by the end of the day.
- We can't go on without an agreement on this crucial point.
- There must be a way out of this sticky situation. Let's find it.
- We can't move forward without coming to grips with the current problem.
- To solve this problem, we need to immediately change tactics.
- I think we can all agree that we need a quick solution to this problem.
- We need to fix this as quickly as possible.
- In order for the problem to be solved quickly, we must work together.
- Our priority is getting to the heart of the issue as soon as possible.
- The more practical we are, the more ground we can cover.
- Let's think outside the box for a moment.
- Since what we've been doing isn't helping, what if we....
- This approach isn't working. We need to try something different.
- I think we need more clarity on the issue.
- We need to rethink that solution.
- What a quandary! How do we get out of it?
- The only way out is to deal with this issue in greater depth.

LAISSEZ-FAIRE

- There's only one way around this, and that's through it.
- Let's settle on a solution that we can all be comfortable with.
- Rather than getting off track, we should work together to find a solution.
- We need more facts about the situation before we do anything.
- We're not getting much done this way. Why not try something else?
- What if we took this in a different direction?
- It's time to get better acquainted with this problem, so I suggest...
- We have been doing this when we should have been...
- Doing the same thing repeatedly and expecting different results is the definition of insanity.
- If we're not part of the solution, we're part of the problem.
- The way forward is to dig deeper, not rush to a solution.
- Let's not rush this—better safe than sorry.
- The worst thing we could do is put a temporary band-aid on the issue.
- I want a comprehensive solution, not a temporary fix.
- Why don't we all sleep on it and reconvene tomorrow?
- Maybe we should let the problem solve itself.
- Sometimes doing nothing is the best solution.

How to Ask Someone for Help

PROFESSIONAL

CASUAL

- Would you be so kind as to render your assistance on this matter?
- I apologise for the interruption, but I really could use your help.
- I can't see an end to this project—would you be willing to lend a hand?
- Do you mind helping me sort out this mess?
- I'm in dire need of your expertise—do you have a moment?
- I don't yet know how I am going to fix this; do you have any ideas?
- I need to find a solution to this problem; what are your thoughts?
- You may hold the key to the answer.
- Help me find the proper solution to the problem.
- I'd appreciate it if you would help me out with this— I'm stumped!
- I need your support or I'll never get out of this dilemma.
- This seems to be slipping through my fingers—maybe you can do better?
- I'll listen to any input you might have.
- I'd love it if you proposed a solution.
- Would you help me out, please?
- Can you give me some support on this?
- What do you propose as a solution?
- If only you could help me get out of this bind!
- Do you have a solution to this mess?
- I need your brilliant mind/vast experience to help me figure this out.
- Help me out, here!
- Care to take a crack at it?

How to Simplify a Complex Issue

DIPLOMATIC

- I'm afraid this is too complex for me—would you be so kind as to simplify the matter?
- Let's keep this simple: what exactly do you mean?
- Is there any way you can outline just the salient facts?
- I wish I could grasp what you are saying, but I can't.
- I'm afraid your complex approach is far too sophisticated for me.
- Would you streamline your thoughts? I'm having trouble getting your point.
- Please don't get too complicated. I'm better when things are stripped down.
- I like to keep things simple—how about you?
- Just the main points, please
- The more concise the dialogue, the better.
- Simplicity is the best course for now.
- Let's stick to the basics, okay?
- I'm afraid this is all over my head.
- Why do you want to go over all that right now?
- Let's stay within the basic framework of the issue.
- Let's not complicate matters unnecessarily.
- Let's not go down useless tangents and dead-ends.
- Let's be more brief, shall we?
- Please confine yourself to the fundamentals.
- The details aren't important—let's just go over the basics.
- Tell me exactly what's going on in 25 words or less.
- Just give me the basic outline of the issue.
- This is getting way too complex for me—can we start over?

RUDE

- This issue would be more easily understood if we kept things straightforward.
- I only have a few minutes, so get to the point.
- Just the facts, ma'am [joking]
- Cut to the chase—I don't have a lot of time.
- You're killing me with all the excruciating minutiae.
- Remember, KISS means "keep it simple, stupid."
- Can you just get on with it?
- Cut out the useless babble!

How to Speak to Someone Who's Going Through a Hard Time

PERSONAL

- How can I best help you during this difficult time?
- I am really concerned about you and I want to help in whatever way I can.
- I am here for you if you need anything at all.
- I have been where you are now and I completely understand.
- I hear you and feel your pain.
- While it is easy to feel helpless in times like these, let me assure you that...
- I believe we can overcome anything by talking things through.
- This, too, shall pass.
- Let's face it, life is hard.
- Life sure has a way of blindsiding you, doesn't it?
- We can't escape reality, as much as we want to.
- We all have to carry on despite personal problems.
- In moments like these, we must be strong.
- That which doesn't kill you makes you stronger.

LESS ENGAGED

- You just need to accept what you can't change.
- Everyone goes through tough times; you're no different.
- Well, they say that everything happens for a reason.
- Oh, you will be fine, I just know it.
- Nobody has a corner on suffering, you know.
- Buck up—it'll get better.

How to Talk About a Current Problem

POSITIVE

- Let's go over what needs to be dealt with and fix it.
- I believe we can overcome anything by talking things through.
- We can overcome this challenge if we work together.
- We should go over the details to deal with this situation better.
- A discussion needs to happen in order for us to get out of this quagmire.
- We can solve this brain teaser if we put our heads together.
- Let's take another look at the problem.
- We need to discuss things further. Do you have a minute?
- Sure we're in a dilemma. Discussing our options will help.
- Perhaps if we talk more we can sort it all out.
- We should get better acquainted with this challenge.
- We have a lot to learn and not a lot of time. Let's get to the bottom of it.
- What's happening isn't making anything easier. Let's discuss it.
- This discussion should help somehow.

- If we don't work quickly, there will be a lot more trouble downstream.
- We've got a real problem if we can't clean this up soon.
- If we don't solve this quickly it's going to lead to more serious trouble.
- We can't afford to let the situation get any worse.
- We can't let the situation boil over.
- Without direct immediate action, the problem will only get worse.
- This problem isn't going to solve itself.
- We're on the verge of disaster, here!
- The Titanic is sinking and nobody seems to care!

NEGATIVE

How to Talk About a Past Problem

- We learned a lot from that and are stronger for it.
- Those hard times are what made us what we are today.
- Thankfully, all of that drama is behind us now.
- That which did not kill us just made us stronger.
- That challenge already seems like it's part of the distant past.
- The troubles we faced are already in the rearview mirror.
- Fortunately, we're past all that now.
- The issues of the past only make us wiser in the present.
- We faced difficult challenges, but we always knew we'd overcome them.
- The problems we encountered will be relegated to the history books.

POSITIVE

NEGATIVE

- We learned a great deal from that, but we need to look to the future.
- We can't erase the past, but we can make a better future.
- While our troubles are behind us, no one escaped unscathed.
- If you don't learn from history you are doomed to repeat it.
- Unfortunately we cannot rewrite the past.
- What's done is done; we just need to move on.
- We didn't handle that well; we need to do better next time.
- Sometimes it seems like we're doomed to repeat our past failures.

How to Propose a Plan

ASSERTIVE

- I believe my plan gives us the best chance for success.
- I think you'll agree that my plan is the best choice.
- The only option is to listen to my suggestion.
- Experience tells me that my plan will lead us down the right path.
- If we look at my new idea, I think we can accomplish a lot more.
- Let's try something new!
- We need a new direction; who's with me?
- I would like to introduce an idea into the mix.
- There's a new direction I'd like to propose.
- How about we do it this way?
- Only thorough planning can help us succeed.
- Please consider using my plan—I think it will help.
- We've pondered many options, but I'm in favor of...

PASSIVE

- Our choices are never easy. That's why I'm in favor of...
- I have no other choice than to suggest...
- I guess we can try my plan if you want.
- This probably won't work, but...
- It's probably hopeless, but...

When You Need Calm

FORMAL

- Please, let's all work together in a spirit of tolerance.
- We can stay focused if we all just calm down.
- We have to demonstrate that we can keep to the straight and narrow.
- Maybe we should regroup and get our thoughts together.
- We must concentrate on the task at hand.
- We must keep the peace to keep moving in the right direction.
- The emphasis must be on the work, not our differences.
- I'm asking everyone to remain calm.
- Everybody take a deep breath, please.
- Please stay calm—we need to find solutions.
- This is no time to fly off the handle.
- I can't keep my concentration with all this static.
- It's impossible to hear yourself think with all this commotion.
- I can't work in all this upheaval.
- Let's not lose our heads over this.
- Everyone keep the peace.
- Settle down, everybody!
- Be still, everyone!
- Keep cool, everyone!

CASUAL

- Don't get your knickers in a twist!
- Everyone, just calm down/pipe down/shut up!

How to Warn Someone

SUBTLE

BOLD

- Are you sure you want to do that?
- You probably don't want to do that.
- Maybe you should rethink this/sleep on it.
- I just want to be sure you know what you're getting yourself into.
- I'm aware that you know what you're doing, but please rethink this.
- I would not advise you to...
- I would suggest that you...
- Wouldn't it be more rational to...
- Do you think it's possible that this is a bad idea?
- Only fools rush in.
- I'm begging you to please avoid this.
- Here's what you're in for if you go that route.
- This does not portend good things for you.
- This certainly won't bode well for you.
- This won't end well.
- With that kind of mindset, prepare yourself for the worst.
- Don't come crying to me if things don't work out.
- I'm not responsible if things blow up in your face.
- I don't want to say, "I told you so."
- Terrible idea—don't say I didn't warn you.

How to Complain

CIVIL

- If I did not care, I would not say anything about it.
- I want to give you the opportunity to address my concerns.
- You're doing well, but here is where you can improve.
- I'm usually not one to complain—are *you* happy with things?
- Look at it from my point of view...

- I don't want to be disrespectful, but this just isn't right.
- I don't want to make a fuss, but this isn't working for me.
- I normally don't whine, but I have to make an exception.
- I usually don't gripe about things, but this has gone too far.
- Don't you have a problem with what happened?
- You may be okay with this, but I'm not.
- If you cared about my feelings, you'd change this.
- I object to/am disappointed in the way you...
- I have a bone to pick with you.
- This isn't the right way to treat people.
- This will never do.
- This is completely unacceptable.
- You have completely lost my respect.
- I'm just about done here.
- You screwed up royally.
- I no longer wish to do business with you/stay married to you/work for you.

BLUNT

How to Respond to a Complaint

EMPATHETIC

- If you're unhappy, I'm unhappy.
- If I had to deal with what you are describing, I would be upset, too.
- I understand your concerns and I promise I will resolve things to your satisfaction.
- I agree that this was terrible—I promise I will make it better.
- I understand why you would feel that way—I will do what I can to address it.

- I will not give up until you are completely satisfied.
- I want to know everything so I can correct the problem immediately.
- Help me understand the issue so I can give you my best help.
- Now that I understand what's bothering you I can begin to address it.
- We'll do everything to fix this as soon as possible.
- Sorry about all that—we're working on it.
- Please understand, this was completely unintentional.
- Let me assure you that this is the exception, not the rule.
- I understand your problem, but we can only do so much.
- This isn't my fault, but I'm doing my best to make things better.
- You'll have to be patient. I'm checking with my superiors.
- There is nothing I can do for you right now.
- It's very easy to assume when we don't know.
- I can't do much to help when somebody is talking this way.
- Don't be so unpleasant—I'm doing the best I can.
- Complaining isn't very constructive, you know.
- Your complaint isn't top priority right now.
- Shouting/your attitude isn't making anything better.
- Nobody's perfect.
- Not my problem.
- I don't care.

BOLD

When Someone Is Being Negative

SYMPATHETIC

- I totally understand what you're saying and agree that you have a right to be upset.
- I'm sorry you're having a bad day—what can I do to help?
- I know it's tough, but let's try to stay positive.
- Let's start today by turning our negatives into positives.
- Let's focus on being constructive, okay?
- I know you're having a rough day, but...
- Every problem has a solution, you know.
- So what are you going to do about it? What's your plan?
- Sure there's a problem, but you need to push through it.
- Remember that your attitude has an effect on morale.
- This kind of talk is making things worse than they really are.
- Why are we even talking about that?
- Don't you think you're exaggerating a little?
- Feelings aren't facts.
- Are you going to be in this kind of a mood all day?
- Come on, you're not being very professional/helpful/easy to live with.
- You're letting this get the best of you.
- We're catching your negative vibe like a virus.
- Whining never accomplished anything.
- This is no time to be pessimistic.
- Don't embrace the negative.
- You're just being a defeatist.

UNSYMPATHETIC

- A lot of people have it much worse.
- You're making a big deal out of nothing.
- This isn't the time or the place for that kind of chatter.
- You're harshing everyone's mellow.
- You're bringing down the energy of this place.
- Please, don't add your personal problems into the mix.
- Your cynicism/negativity is making me depressed/ tense/upset.
- I'm really not in the mood for this right now.
- I've heard just about enough of that from you.
- Should we all throw a pity party for you? [sarcasm]
- Should we call you Eeyore? [sarcasm]
- That's life—get over it.
- I feel exhausted just listening to you.
- Please just put a lid on it.

When Someone Is Oversimplifying a Complex Topic

COURTEOUS

- This might be a *bit* more complex than the way you're describing it.
- I think there's more than one side to this issue.
- I understand the advantage of boiling things down to their essence; however...
- In reality, the issue is a lot more complex, don't you think?
- A more sophisticated inquiry into the issue might be more helpful.
- God is in the details.

BLUNT

- Cutting a complex issue down to its component parts is not always wise.
- You cut to the chase almost before the movie began.
- You can't simplify things to such an extreme.
- That's basically the stripped down version of the issue.
- You can't prune everything off and still expect it to be a tree.
- I think you're dumbing this down.
- That's a myopic way of looking at it.

Courtesy

Courtesy is as much a mark of a gentleman as courage.
—Theodore Roosevelt

Even when there's no crisis, leaders must project their capability and charisma in the more mundane aspects of life, such as common courtesy. This is an area that can humble even the most dynamic leader because it can catch one off guard. To wit, here are a few tips to help you lead with courtesy:

1. Treat others as you want to be treated

You've undoubtedly seen it once or twice before: someone at your workplace unloads on someone else, using the imperative tense and a tone of voice that is simply outrageous. Did this help either person? Certainly not. A little courtesy, not to mention empathy and respect, would have served both of them better. If you find yourself in this position, take a deep breath, excuse yourself to calm down, and reconvene when the matter can be discussed more calmly and constructively—and courteously.

2. Smile

A simple smile goes a long way toward establishing you as an affable and approachable person. In fact, smiling is a great source of stress relief. Whenever you smile, others are likely to smile with you, effectively spreading the joy. Contrary to popular opinion, truly great leaders don't cultivate an unapproachable, testy, or even intimidating demeanor.

3. Be inclusive

People who are gifted at courteous conversation typically have an inclusive perspective, regardless of the other person's point of view or how it's expressed. Being inclusive means that a real leader will avoid discriminatory or sexist language. So for example, instead of saying "policeman" say "police officer," and instead of "stewardess" say "flight attendant." Language has the power to shape your life as well as the lives of those around you.

4. Use body language and tone of voice to your advantage

Body language is something you're going to need to master if you hope to be an effective communicator. John Borg states that human communication consists of 93 percent body language and paralinguistic cues, while only 7 percent of communication consists of the words themselves (Borg, *Body Language: 7 Easy Lessons to Master the Silent Language*, Prentice Hall Life, 2008). As such, body language can provide the best clues as to the real attitude or state of mind of a person. Examine the way you use your body in front of a mirror, or better yet, videotape yourself and then play it back (warning: you might be shocked at what you see!). Keep your gestures under control and look straight at the person or persons you're talking to. Also maintain a medium good voice level and avoid emotional outbursts that take you off track and undermine your strategies.

5. Avoid gossip

While it can be exciting to share juicy tidbits around the copy machine or the water cooler, it can really hurt you if your statements get back to the person(s) concerned. Although you may feel as though you are bonding with others, your gossip will make the people around you uneasy, even if they don't say so out loud. A truly courteous person will not talk trash about others. This will also have the effect of engendering trust in others: they know you don't talk about others, so it's likely you won't talk about them, either.

6. Don't interrupt

If you tend to cut people off, you will be perceived as rude, argumentative, and egotistical, none of which will help your position as a leader. A truly courteous person always allows others to finish making their point before speaking. If you have two or more questions to interject, write them down and then refer to the list once you have the floor.

How to Ask for Help

FORMAL

CASUAL

- Would you be so kind as to render your assistance in this matter?
- I would be grateful for any help you could offer.
- I would hold your offer of help in the highest regard.
- Far be it from me to bother you, but would you...?
- You're certainly under no obligation, but would you...?
- Only when you get a chance, would you...?
- When you have a moment, would you...?
- If it doesn't take too much time, would you please...?
- I was wondering if you would possibly...?
- Helping me right now would be the ultimate act of kindness.
- Please help me get through this minor catastrophe.
- I would appreciate a little assistance with this.
- Would you mind helping me with this? It shouldn't take long.
- If you're okay with it, would you please...?
- Would you please lend me a hand?
- I need a favor, please!
- Do me a solid, won't you?
- I'll owe you one for sure.
- You know I'd do it for you! [joking]
- Man overboard! [joking]

How to Offer Your Help

FORMAL

CASUAL

- I am, as always, at your disposal.
- Please allow me to be of assistance.
- Ask and you shall receive.
- If you should ever need my help, please feel free to let me know.
- How can I best help you?
- I'm here to support you in any way I can.
- You can always count on me.
- What kind of friend would I be if I didn't help you?
- I know you would do it for me.
- Is there anything I can do?
- Let me know if I can do anything, okay?
- Do you need a hand with that?
- You look like you could use some help—am I right?
- I can help you but it's going to cost you. [joking]
- If I didn't help you, how could I sleep at night? [joking]
- Give a holler if you need anything, okay?

When Someone Asks You for Help

EMPATHETIC

- I would be delighted to assist you in this matter.
- Of course, I'd love to!
- I was hoping you'd ask.
- I'd be glad to help.
- You can always count on me.
- There's no need to ask me twice.
- You're always there for me, aren't you?
- I guess I can try to help.

REJECTING

- Okay, but I probably won't be of much help to you.
- I'll see what I can do, but don't get your hopes up.
- Okay, but you really owe me one.
- I regret that I can't be of assistance in this matter.
- I'd love to help you but I just can't right now.
- I'd like to but I'm already up to my neck.
- I don't have the time, unfortunately.
- I'm going to have to decline.
- I don't think that's something that I'm going to do.
- Why should I?
- You need to figure it out yourself.
- Have you ever heard of learned helplessness?
- Get lost!

How to Thank Someone

PROFESSIONAL

- I very much appreciate everything you've done.
- I greatly appreciate all your efforts.
- Thank you so much.
- I am eternally in your debt.
- There's no way to thank you enough.
- How can I ever express my gratitude?
- Words cannot describe how grateful I am.
- I'm so grateful for all you've done.
- How can I thank you for all your hard work?
- People like you are a rarity these days.
- I don't think anyone else could have helped as much as you.
- I would like to thank you from the bottom of my heart.
- Without your help I would have been floundering.

CASUAL

- I really appreciate all you've done for me.
- That was very kind of you.
- I owe you one.
- You're a gem, thanks!
- You rock!

When Someone Thanks You

FORMAL

- You are most welcome.
- I'm glad I could help.
- It was the very least I could do.
- I am so glad I could be of service.
- I would do it again in a heartbeat.
- If you're happy, I'm happy.
- It's always a pleasure.
- My pleasure.
- No problem.
- Happy to help.
- You bet!
- Pray, don't mention it. [joking]
- Ah, it was nothing. [joking]
- Next time, I'll charge you! [joking]

CASUAL

How to Compliment Someone

FORMAL

- I admire you greatly.
- I think so highly of you.
- People like you are a rarity.
- You're someone I would like to emulate.
- You're obviously a person of great skill/intelligence/ experience.
- You always strive for excellence.
- You are so impressive.
- I admire you so much.

CASUAL

- I take my hat off to you.
- You're a real mover and a shaker.
- You're one of a kind.
- I think you're awesome.
- You're a winner.
- You're a real go-getter.
- You're the best.
- You are my hero.
- If I could be anyone else, it would be you. [joking]
- I wish I could be you for a day. [joking]
- You're great.
- You're awesome.
- You rock!

When Someone Compliments You

ACCEPTING

- Tell me something I didn't already know.
- Yes, I am fabulous, aren't I?
- How kind of you to say so.
- Thank you, that's very nice of you to say.
- Thank you for the compliment.
- That is praise indeed, coming from you.
- Oh stop, before my head gets too big. [joking]
- Ah, it takes one to know one. [joking]
- I truly appreciate that.
- I don't know what to say.
- Flattery will get you nowhere. [joking]
- Stop, you're making me blush.
- I can't take all the credit, you know.
- It wasn't just me—I had a great deal of help.
- There's no "I" in "team."

DEFLECTING

- I can't take credit for that, but thank you.
- I really can't take credit for it.
- I'd do the same thing even if no one were around to notice.
- I only did what any ordinary person would do.
- I don't deserve such flattery.
- Oh, it was nothing special/no big deal.
- C'mon, that's not true.

When Someone Invites You

ACCEPTING

- Thank you so much for thinking of me.
- I would be honored to attend.
- I'd love to come.
- You can count on me to be there.
- There's nowhere else I'd rather be.
- Thank you so much for the invitation—I'd be delighted.
- I will be there with bells on.
- Consider this my R.S.V.P.!
- You don't have to ask me twice.
- I've already got it marked down in my book/calendar.
- I'd like to be there—is the agenda/guest list set yet?
- I'd like to attend. Would you e-mail me the details?
- I can only accept if I know a little more about the event.
- I'd like to but I need to check my calendar.
- I really don't want to double book, so let me check.
- I have a lot going on right now. Can I get back to you tomorrow?
- I'm so busy these days—not sure if I can make it.
- If it was on another day, maybe.
- Probably not—I'll have to get back to you.
- Unfortunately I can't break free, not even for a moment.
- Unfortunately I have previous engagement.

REJECTING

- I hate to turn you down, but I'm tapped out these days.
- I'd like to, but I have something else going on.
- I have to give you my regrets—but I'm sure you'll have a great time without me!
- I'm tied up that day, sorry.
- I just don't have time for a social life these days.

How to Apologize for Something You Said

HUMBLE

- There's no excuse for what I said; please forgive me.
- I really have knack for saying the wrong thing. I am so sorry.
- Please let me apologize; that was an awful thing to say.
- I always put my foot in my mouth, it seems; please forgive me.
- Clearly, I wasn't thinking clearly when I said that. I apologize.
- I feel horrible about what I said; let me make it up to you.
- I wish I could take it all back; I feel terrible.
- I spoke without thinking—can I have a do-over?
- I feel like a complete klutz about what I said.
- What I said was wrong, I admit it.
- I recognize that I stepped out of bounds with that remark.
- Please allow me to rectify the situation.
- I'd like to restate that, please.
- May I retract my statement?
- I can't believe I said that.
- I didn't mean any harm, you know.
- Let me rephrase that/take it back.
- If I crossed the line, I apologize
- There's no excuse for what was said.
- I didn't think you were going to take it so personally, sorry.
- I was just having a bad day.

- My tongue got the better of me.
- Please pay no mind to what I said.
- Whoa—did I say that out loud?
- I guess I had a lapse in judgment.
- I think I had my brain in neutral when I said that. [joking]
- I apologise if I misspoke or hurt your feelings in any way.
- Accept my apologies if what I said was wrong.
- I said what I said because you caught me off guard.
- I know I made a mistake, but I'm only human.
- Have you never made a mistake?
- Don't be so sensitive.

ARROGANT

How to Apologise for Something You Did

- Please forgive me; there is no excuse for my actions.
- My actions were inexcusable; please forgive me.
- I really made a mess of things; I hope you can forgive me.
- I am sorry I did you wrong—please allow me to make it up to you.
- I regret it and I promise it will never happen again.
- I can't tell you how sorry I am for what I did.
- I hope you can forgive me for my thoughtlessness.
- Words can't express how much I regret my actions.
- I never, ever meant to hurt/disrespect you.
- Hurting you was the last thing on my mind.
- Even though I'm sorry, I know that won't make it go away.
- Obviously I regret what I did, even if I didn't know it was wrong.
- I guess I just wasn't thinking.
- I'll try to never do that again.
- I feel badly, but I can't undo what I did, unfortunately.

HUMBLE

ARROGANT

- There are a lot of things I would do differently if I could.
- If I stepped on your toes/hurt you/offended you, I apologize.
- I'm sorry if I hurt you.
- Listen, I'm only human.
- I feel wretched, but haven't you ever made a mistake?
- I didn't do it on purpose!
- *Mea culpa.* [sarcasm]

How to Apologise for Forgetting Something

HUMBLE

- It was inexcusable of me to forget; I humbly apologize.
- It is so unlike me to be this forgetful; it will never happen again.
- If I could turn back the hands of time, I would.
- Words cannot express how badly I feel.
- I'm so thoughtless to have forgotten.
- Can you ever forgive me for being so distracted?
- I'm usually very organized; I don't know how this happened.
- I just can't believe this slipped my mind.
- I don't know what I was thinking.
- I apologize; I'm just a lame brain.
- You know me—I'm just a flake.
- Please forgive me—I simply didn't remember.
- I can't help it if I'm so forgetful.

ARROGANT

- I just get a little absentminded from time to time.
- Don't get on my case; it was an oversight and nothing more.
- Have you never forgotten anything in your life?

How to Apologize for Being Late

HUMBLE

ARROGANT

- I'm so sorry for being late; I won't let it happen again!
- Thank you for waiting; I apologize for my tardiness.
- I have no valid reason for keeping you waiting; please forgive me.
- There is absolutely no justification for my tardiness.
- I have no excuse; I should have planned ahead.
- I always strive to be punctual; I don't know what happened.
- This isn't like me; I'm never late.
- Yes I was late, but I'll make it up to you
- I guess it's time for me to buy a watch! [joking]
- Thanks for your patience.
- I understand if you never want to meet me again! (joking)
- I hope you weren't standing here too long
- I'm late because my life is so hectic; I'm sure you understand.
- I know it's a lame excuse, but things have been hectic lately.
- Excuse my lateness: [insert random excuse here].
- You know me: I'm always 10 minutes late for everything.
- Punctuality was never my forte.
- It seems I'm always falling behind
- I know I'm late, but so what?
- Have you never been late in your life?
- It's a wonder that you'll ever meet with me again. [sarcasm]

How to Apologize for Your Team's Mistake

HUMBLE

- I am personally responsible for what transpired.
- It was my fault; it will never happen on my watch again.
- I know that we dropped the ball, and for that I apologise.
- I am tremendously sorry for what occurred; this team will make up for it in full.
- I apologize for the inconvenience; what can we do to make up for it?
- If there's anything we can do, this team is equipped to fix this.
- We are disturbed this happened and are deeply sorry for any damages.
- We fully guarantee that this mishap will never repeat itself.
- I'm fully aware of the situation and we're working on it now.
- We will definitely be more careful in the future.
- Please rest assured that we have learned from our mistake.
- Please know we are doing everything we can to fix this.
- I apologize on behalf of the team for any errors that might have been made.
- I admit that we've been far from perfect.
- My group must take responsibility for its actions.
- As a group, we are ashamed of what occurred and take full responsibility.

ARROGANT

- We've certainly made more than our share of mistakes.
- Our mistake was never intentional.
- Other than apologize, I don't know what else we can do.
- We are sorry for the inconvenience—what else do you want?
- This kind of mistake happens all time.
- Nobody's perfect.

Machiavellian Techniques

It is better to be feared than loved, if you cannot be both.
—Niccoló Machiavelli

Over the years, the adjective *Machiavellian* has become a term describing someone who manipulates others for personal advantage. A Machiavellian leader is often ingenious and insightful, although his tactics may seem ethically suspect to some. A true Machiavellian often has the reputation for being a cunning, sly master of social engineering. Of course, not every great leader could be considered Machiavellian, but some find that a judicious use of these tactics can be effective. But beware: you'll not endear yourself to others if you use these tactics!

1. Intimidate

If people are approaching you with a certain fear, uncertainty, or doubt, you're more than halfway to winning. Demonstrate that you always have higher priorities than what others are asking from you.

2. Build a firewall

Build an impenetrable wall around yourself and keep most people outside of it. Limit their access and frustrate their efforts to get to you. This will make them angry, but it will allow you to maneuver without encumbrance. Like a sailboat in a race, you can only maintain your top speed if you get rid of the barnacles that encrust your hull. By doing this, you will also be less likely to take the feelings of others into account, which is very Machiavellian.

3. Motivate

Freud said that people do things for two reasons: to obtain pleasure or to avoid pain. The Machiavellian knows how to leverage both the carrot and the stick to his/her advantage. A properly motivated employee works faster, requires less direction, and actually takes more pride in what he or she accomplishes.

4. Keep social climbers away from you

If you are successful, regardless of how you got to the top, you will be surrounded by social climbers. Limit access to yourself with a "recommend only" principle. If a newcomer arrives to you without being recommended by someone you trust, he/she doesn't get an audience. Period. Making it difficult for others to get an audience with you will also increase your value in their eyes.

How to Destabilize Someone

SUBTLE

OVERT

- Would you repeat yourself, please?
- I'm sorry—what did you say?
- Hold on, I need to write this down.
- What is your name again?
- What is your reason for saying that?
- Why would you believe that?
- What makes you say that?
- What are you trying to say?
- How did you come to that conclusion?
- I'm not following you at all.
- I really wonder why you would think this.
- How can you be so sure?
- You don't seem 100-percent sure of yourself.
- Would you bet your life on it?
- So you say.
- That's what you think.
- Interesting...
- Whatever...

How to Threaten Someone

SUBTLE

- I'm not sure where this leaves us.
- You might not want to do that.
- I don't think that's the best idea.
- You really should rethink your approach to this.
- I don't think it's healthy for you to continue on this track.
- For every action, there is an equal and opposite reaction.
- You do know there are consequences to every action, right?

OVERT

- You are responsible for yourself from here on out.
- I would advise you not to do that.
- You're going to regret that
- I'm warning you, there are consequences to every action.
- Please stop before you say/do something you'll really regret.
- You should prepare yourself for the worst.
- Have you ever heard of Karma?
- Someone's going to cut you down to size one day.
- Your punishment will come in time.
- Bad things happen to bad people, you know.
- You're going to pay dearly for that.
- This is it for you!
- You'd better not stop looking over your shoulder.

How to Extract Information From Someone

SUBTLE

- I promise, anything you say will remain completely confidential.
- I am as silent as the grave.
- You know you can tell me anything.
- This is just between the two of us.
- I give you my word that this won't go any further than these walls.
- Word on the street says you know what's going on.
- You know that we have an understanding.
- I just need you to help me connect the dots.
- Can we cut to the chase?
- It would be nice to get it straight from the horse's mouth.
- I guess I'll have to call around to get the facts.

OVERT

- You know I would tell *you* if the situation were reversed.
- I'm going to find out anyway, so you might as well tell me.
- I can go behind your back or I can get it directly from you; your call.
- Don't you trust me?
- Why are you holding back on me?
- I'm hurt that you wouldn't trust me with this information.
- What have you got to hide?
- I'm not asking about anything that isn't common knowledge.
- I have all day to wait so why not just tell me?
- I'm not leaving here without the information
- It would go much better for you if you just cooperated.
- Cut the crap and give me the answers I want!
- Maybe you'd prefer that I beat it out of you? [joking]

How to Deflect Blame

HIGH ROAD

- What you say is simply not true.
- I am prepared to defend myself against these allegations.
- If there is anyone who can categorically state that I did/said this, let him/her step forward.
- I know a dozen people who will vouch for me.
- I'm actually hurt that you would accuse me of something like that.
- The energy you're using to blame me could be used in much more constructive ways.
- This is simply the result of rumor and innuendo.
- These accusations are the work of a desperate person.
- Do you really think I would say/do something like that?

LOW ROAD

- Why would I do something like that?
- I swear on a stack of Bibles that I didn't do it.
- It wasn't me.
- *My* conscience is clear.
- I don't deserve this.
- Before you attack me, you should look in the mirror.
- These accusations are utter B.S.
- Blaming me is the way you deflect blame from yourself.
- The more you try to trap me, the more you point the finger at yourself.
- Your statements make it clear that you are incompetent.

How to Make Someone Feel Like a Fool

HUMOROUS

- Please turn your mouth off; I can still hear it running. [joking]
- The jerk store called and they're running out of you. [joking]
- Aw, you try so hard.
- Aren't you cute.
- Okaaaaay....[dubious]
- Really?
- Do you always do stuff like this?
- Wow, that's an...*interesting* outfit/idea/thought.
- I know you like to help, but I think we've got things under control.
- You remind me a lot of me when I was young and ignorant.
- I won't have a battle of wits with an unarmed opponent.
- You, my friend, are suffering from delusions of adequacy.

- I hope you're better prepared today.
- The sign on the door reads, "Professionals only."
- I'd love to hear something intelligent for a change.
- When I need your opinion, I'll ask for it.
- I don't have to make you feel stupid; you're halfway there on your own.
- I liked what you just said very much—at least the parts that made sense. [sarcasm]
- I'll try being nicer if you'll try being smarter. [sarcasm]
- I need your help like a dog needs a tick. [sarcasm]
- I didn't hear you—my B.S. filter was on. [sarcasm]
- How many times do I have to flush before you go away?
- How do you sleep at night?

HARSH

When Someone Is Meddling in Your Business

- Too many cooks spoil the broth. [joking]
- Hey, I called dibs on this job first. [joking]
- I've got it covered—thank you, though.
- I think this is a one-person operation.
- Thanks, but I think I have a handle on it.
- I have this covered already.
- I assume you've already done the jobs you were assigned?
- Maybe there is something else you can do.
- A little breathing room, please?
- Maybe you should worry about your own stuff.
- Please don't get involved in things that don't concern you.
- Don't you have something else you need to do/ somewhere else you need to be?
- Don't you have anything better to do?

FRIENDLY

FORCEFUL

- Why don't you take care of your side of the street instead?
- Would you please grace this space with your absence?
- I've got things under control, but thanks. [sarcasm]
- Um, who invited you to this party?
- Get lost.

How to Take Control of a Conversation

POLITE

- If you would allow me to speak for a moment...
- Perhaps you didn't understand me.
- May I just say this?
- Excuse me, I'm not finished.
- I haven't finished what I was saying.
- Pardon me!
- There's really no need for you to go on.
- I think I've heard enough.
- This case is closed.
- Someone needs to stop beating this dead horse.
- There simply isn't anything more to say on the matter.
- Your reasoning is going nowhere.
- You're wasting your time and energy.
- What kind of mentality is that?
- Didn't your family teach you respect?
- I think you've said enough already.
- I'd be more than happy to let you ramble on, but I've got more important things to do.
- I'm done listening to you; now it's your turn to hear me out.
- What part of "done" don't you understand? [sarcasm]

BLUNT

- No offense, but would you please just shut up?
- Just FYI: I will be controlling this conversation from now on.

How to Get The Last Word In

SUBTLE

- Yes, but...
- I agree, but...
- You may be right, but...
- So you say.
- Okay, whatever. [repeat as necessary]
- Before we finish, let me just say one last thing.
- Let me just say one more thing and then we're done.
- Okay, but I'm not letting this go.
- We'll continue this at a later date of my choosing.
- We'll talk more about this later/tomorrow/some other time.
- I will follow up about this later/tomorrow/next week.
- No, I'm done here for now.
- Okay, I guess I'd better let you go.
- Here is my summation of the issue as I see it.
- Let's wrap it up; there's really nothing more to say.
- That may be the long and the short of it, but it's not the end of it.
- You've talked enough, thank you.
- Now you're just repeating yourself.
- I'm not going to change my mind, so it's best that you stop talking.

OVERT

- This is the last thing I want to say and then this conversation is finished.

How to Make People Second-Guess Themselves

SUBTLE

- I know you mean well.
- I'm sure you're doing the best you can.
- How could you have known?
- Hmm, that's not what I heard.
- Hmm, you might want to consider the source.

- I was led to believe something quite different.
- That's not what so-and-so told me.
- Where did you get your information?
- I'm curious—what were you thinking?
- Why would you do/say something like that?
- Aren't you angry/upset about that?
- If I were you, I'd be pretty P.O.'d.
- Sometimes I just don't get you.
- You mean you didn't know that...?
- It's a shame you didn't know about this.
- It's usually pretty obvious what you're thinking.
- Honestly I'm a bit surprised by your attitude/actions.
- If I were you, I would be so mad/upset/sad/hurt.
- Nobody else I know thinks that.
- How can you tolerate that?
- This is not really what I expected from you.
- I'm really not sure why you're reacting that way.
- That's not how I would have done it, but whatever.
- I'm sure you know what's best.... [dubious]

How to Avoid a Conversation

- Let's set aside this topic and move on to more pressing matters.
- This topic of conversation might be better suited for another day.
- Can we put this off until a later date?
- I think we should discuss this some other time.
- This is a touchy subject—let's steer clear of it.
- This is a controversial subject—probably best to avoid it.
- I don't think we need to address that, but that's just my humble opinion.
- I'm not comfortable talking about this right now, sorry.
- I'm pretty sure we don't need to get into this.

- Perhaps we can just cross that off the agenda.
- There is a bit too much controversy surrounding this conversation.
- That is a subject I don't wish to continue discussing.
- That subject is off limits in my book.
- Maybe we shouldn't talk about such a touchy subject.
- It would be a waste of our time to discuss this any further.
- Why talk about this if we can avoid it?
- I don't believe that this is important.
- Is this really important enough to continue discussing?
- The best way to talk about this is to not mention it at all.
- I could talk to you about this, but why waste everyone's time?
- I hope you realize that this topic is a sensitive one.
- You're getting into a big subject, here.
- Maybe we should just table this discussion...forever.
- This topic is not open for discussion.
- We'd just be beating a dead horse talking about this.
- This discussion will not be happening anytime soon.
- Sorry, but I won't discuss that.
- There will be no further deliberation concerning this.
- This is not open for discussion or debate.
- I'm not going to entertain that notion.
- I'm simply not going to listen to another word.
- I don't want to hear a word about it.
- Just drop it, okay?

UNPROFESSIONAL

How to Evade Someone

DIPLOMATIC

- Wow, everyone wants a piece of me today! [joking]
- I'm sorry, but I've got too many plates in the air at the moment.
- I'd love to talk to you, but I haven't got a minute today.
- I wish I could linger, but duty calls.
- I'll try to catch up to you some other time, I promise.
- I'd like to chat, but I'm just running out the door.
- If you want, you can make an appointment with my secretary.
- I'm so busy—can you shoot me an email/leave a voicemail/talk to my assistant?
- I'd love to hang out, but I'm just on my way out.
- Perhaps we can discuss this some other time?
- I just don't have the time right now, unfortunately.
- I'd rather not discuss that, if that's okay with you.
- I don't want to talk about it now.
- We already talked about this, didn't we?
- Is this conversation really necessary?
- Why stir the pot when we can call it a day?
- Continuing to hash this out isn't productive.
- If you still feel the need to hash it out, please leave a message on my phone.
- I don't wish to ever have that conversation.
- I don't wish to deliberate any further.
- Why should we discuss anything?
- Sorry, I'm really not interested.

RUDE

- Excuse me, but this conversation is not happening.
- Why would I discuss this with *you*? [sarcasm]
- This discussion will never happen—sorry!
- You're the last person on earth I would discuss this with/hang out with.
- Oops, look at the time!
- Take a hike!

How to Engender Trust

ENERGETIC

- I will never let you down.
- My word is my bond.
- I would walk through fire for you.
- When I make a commitment/promise, I always keep it.
- I have a high degree of confidence regarding the situation.
- My integrity is unimpeachable.
- I feel great about this.
- All systems are go.
- Please put your trust in me—I won't let you down.
- I will stop at nothing to make this happen.
- Trust me, it will be taken care of.
- You can trust me, I promise.
- My reputation precedes me.
- Believe in me just as I believe in you.
- I am known for my trustworthiness.
- I have many years of experience in [topic at hand].
- I am a person of integrity, I assure you.
- I tell the truth in all matters.

- Ask around. I have a good reputation.
- I've kept going when others might have stopped.
- I will make every effort to make this happen.
- I feel at peace about the outcome.
- I'll hold myself responsible if things go awry.
- You have no reason to distrust me.
- I have no reason to lie to you, do I?

Bonus Section

How Leaders Say Yes

DEFINITIVE

TENTATIVE

- Absolutely.
- Positively.
- Certainly.
- I agree.
- I concur.
- Of course.
- Precisely.
- Exactly.
- Without a doubt.
- Very much so.
- That's for sure.
- It's a sure thing.
- That's exactly the case.
- I'm of the same opinion.
- In a word, yes.
- We're of the same mindset.
- We're on the same wavelength.
- We're of one accord on that.
- Hey, you're reading my mind.
- I'm with you on that.
- Message received.
- If I have to give an answer, then it's yes.
- I'm pretty sure that's the case.

How Leaders Say No

DEFINITIVE

TENTATIVE

- Under no circumstances.
- That's out of the question.
- That's impossible.
- Absolutely not.
- I'm sorry, but no.
- No can do.
- I can't agree to that.
- I'm afraid that's not an option.
- I have to humbly disagree.
- I'm going to have to respectfully decline.
- I wouldn't necessarily say that.
- I don't get that impression
- Not to my knowledge.
- It doesn't seem that way to me.
- It doesn't make sense to me.
- I tend to disagree.
- I don't think so.
- That wouldn't be my preference right now.
- I don't think that's correct, but I could be wrong

How Leaders Say Maybe

FORMAL

- Perhaps.
- That's debatable.
- It's not implausible.
- It's not outside the realm of possibilities.
- It's completely open for discussion.
- I'm not sure.
- I'm not convinced.
- It's not out of the question.

CASUAL

- I couldn't say for sure.
- I'm not sure on the facts.
- It is worth reflecting upon.
- I could go either way.
- It's possible.
- That's iffy
- That's questionable.
- Who knows?

How Leaders Say I Don't Know

DEFINITIVE

- I have absolutely no idea.
- I'm sorry, but I simply don't know.
- Believe me, I wish I knew.
- I haven't a clue.
- I don't have all the facts to give a qualified response.
- I'm not informed enough to give a precise response.
- I'm not knowledgeable enough to have an opinion on the matter.
- I don't know, but I'll find out.
- Hang on, I'll look it up.
- That's a good question, but I don't yet know the answer.
- I can't say anything definitive either way.
- I will need to do more research.
- I'm going to have to plead ignorance.
- I don't have enough information on the subject.
- I'm not sure—let me find out for you.
- I can't really tell.
- I'm not exactly sure.

TENTATIVE

- I could give an answer, but it wouldn't necessarily be correct.
- I don't have a good answer for that.
- I have no response at this time.
- How can I reply if I don't know what I'm talking about?
- I don't think so, but I am not entirely sure.

How Leaders Say I Don't Understand

POLITE

- I'm sorry, but I'm not sure that I understand you entirely.
- Would you be so kind as to explain that to me once more?
- I'm sorry to say this, but I'm not following you.
- I'm not certain if I understand you properly
- Please help me by clarifying.
- Sorry, my mind can't process information that quickly. [joking]
- I am not sure if I understand where you're going with this.
- I'm probably missing something, here.
- I must read up on the subject.
- I'm not sure what you're trying to say.
- Can you say that again in layperson's terms?
- Am I missing something?
- I don't get it.
- I have *no* clue what you're talking about.
- Well, *I'm* lost.
- What the heck?

RUDE

How Leaders Say It's Confidential

POLITE

- I'm sorry, but I'm not at liberty to talk about that with you.
- I'm sorry, but I can't disclose any information on that topic.
- You'd have to read my mind to find out. [joking]
- I'm under oath to keep silent on that. [joking]
- If I told you I'd have to kill you. [joking]
- That info is classified as Top Secret. [joking]
- Sorry, I am not allowed to disclose that type of information.
- Unfortunately there's no way I can speak openly about this.
- I have to plead the Fifth on that.
- It was told to me in confidence.
- I never break a confidence.
- I don't want to step on any toes, here.
- I'm not the best person to answer that question.
- I'm not in a position to give you a complete answer.
- I would be speaking out of turn if I said anything.
- Some things are better left unsaid.
- I don't think it's appropriate to talk about this.
- Why do you need this information?
- You know very well I can't talk about that.
- Leave it alone.
- It's under wraps.
- It's none of your business.
- You're nosing around where you shouldn't be.
- Keep out of it.
- Why would I talk to you about this?

RUDE

Index

accuse someone, how to, 107-108

accusing, when someone is, 115-116

action, how to propose an, 57-58

advice, unwanted, 114-115

agree, how to, 22

anger and conflicts, 71-100
    overview of, 71-73

angry, when someone is, 79-80

apologizing for something you
    did, 161-162

apologizing for something you
    said, 160-161

assigning a task, 52-53

attention, when you need
    someone's full, 51-52

attitude, having a calm, 72

avoiding your question, when
    someone is, 94

bargain, how to, 128-129

blame, how to deflect, 171-172

body language, 152

boss, saying no to your, 46-47

business, when someone is
    meddling in your, 173-174

calling a meeting to order, 54-55

calm, when you need, 143

change the topic, how to, 33-34

changing the topic, when
    someone is, 97-98

clarify a point, how to, 31

communication and compromise, 71

communication, practice, 102

communications ,delegating your, 20

complain, how to, 144-145

complaint, how to respond to a,
    145-146

complex topic, dealing with a,
    148-149

complimenting someone, 157-158

compliments, receiving, 158-159

compromise,
    communication and, 71
    how to call for, 130-131

condescending, when someone is,
    82-83

confide in someone, how to, 32

confidence, how to boost
    someone's, 50

187

confidential, how leaders say it's, 185

conflict between other people,
how to stop a, 75-76

conflicts and anger, 71-100
overview of, 71-73

consensus, how to call a, 108-109

conversation,
general, 19-21
how to ask for a private, 50
how to avoid a, 176-177
how to close a, 25-26
how to defer a, 59-60
how to open a, 24-25
how to refocus a, 56-57
how to take control of a, 174

convince, how to, 124-125

courtesy, 151-165
overview of, 151-153

criticizing you, when someone is, 90-91

debate,
how to open a topic for, 103-104
how to wrap up a, 104-105

decision, how to postpone a, 60-61

defensive, when someone is, 92-93

destabilize someone, how to, 169

diplomacy, 101-117
overview of, 101-102

disagree, how to, 23

doubletalk, the art of, 102

doubting you, when someone is, 93-94

doubts, how to express, 34-35

embarrassing issue, how to bring up an, 49

empathy, listen with, 72-73

employee,
how to fire an, 66-67
how to motivate an, 63-64

engaging the trust of the other side, 101

engender trust, how to, 179-180

extract information from someone, how to, 170-171

falling-out, how to reconnect after, 35-36

fight, when someone picks a, 87-88

finishing your thoughts, 42

firewall, building a, 168

fool, how to make someone feel like a, 172-173

forgetting something, apologizing for, 162

general conversation, overview of, 19-21

gossip, avoiding, 153

help,
how to ask for, 137, 154
how to offer your, 155
when someone asks for your, 155-156

ideas, backing up your, 21

idiom, gaining command of the, 20

inclusive, being, 152

information, how to ask for more, 30

insulting you, when someone is, 98-99

interrupting, 153
when someone is, 88-89

intimidation, importance of, 167-168

invite, accepting an, 159-160

issues, how to simplify, 138-139

justifying yourself, 120

keeping on course, 72

knowledge, backing up your ideas with, 21

last word, how to get the, 175

late, apologizing for being, 163

leader, write like a, 43

lies, when someone, 86-87

listening with empathy, 72-73

Machiavellian techniques, 167-180
overview of, 167-168

makes fun of you, when someone, 89-90

maybe, how leaders say, 182-183

meeting,
calling, 54-55
how to terminate a, 55-56

mistakes, learning from others', 21

misunderstanding, how to get past a, 77

motivation, importance of, 167-168

negative, when someone is being, 147-148

negotiation, 119-131
overview of, 119-120

news, how to share, 26-27

no, how leaders say, 182

offensive statement, how to respond to an, 78-79

opinion,
how to address a difference of, 109-111
how to ask for someone's, 28-29
how to express an, 27-28
how to express an, 29

people, how to unite, 61-62

personal issue,
how to avoid a, 47
how to bring up a, 49

plan, how to propose a, 142-143

point,
how to clarify a, 31
how to emphasize a, 123-124

positively, speaking, 41-42

practice communication, 102

preparing your speeches, 42

pressuring you, when someone is, 80-81

private conversation, how to ask for a, 50

problem solving, 133-149
overview of, 133-134

problem,
how to address a, 135-136
how to talk about a current, 140-141
how to talk about a past, 141-142

proposal,
how to accept a, 125-126
how to reject a, 126-127

public speech, how to open a, 106

question,
how to ask a, 122
when you don't want to answer a, 37-38
when you've answered a, 36-37

raise, how to ask for a, 44-45

reconnecting after a falling-out, 35-36

refocus a conversation, how to, 56-57

repeat yourself, when you are asked to, 39-40

rumors, when you are the subject of, 117

saying no to your boss, 46-47

second-guess, how to make people, 175-176

selling something to someone, 127-128

sensitive topic, how to avoid a, 111-112

slowing things down, 68-69

smiling, importance of, 152

solution, how to propose an, 57-58

someone,
    how to evade, 178-179
    how to thank, 156-157
    how to warn, 144

speak, thinking before you, 42

speaking briefly, 19

speaking clearly, 19

speaking positively, 41-42

speech, how to close a, 107

speeches, preparing your, 42

stalemate, when you are in a, 129

stall, how to, 122-123

stubborn, when someone is being, 81-82

suggestions,
    how to make, 113-114
    unwanted, 114-115

superior, how to flatter a, 62-63

swearing at you, when someone is, 96-97

task,
    assigning a, 52-53
    how to put off a, 58-59

team's mistake, apologizing for your, 164-165

tense situation, how to diffuse a, 74-75

terminate a meeting, how to, 55-56

thanks you, when someone, 157

thinking before you speak, 42

thought, finishing your, 42

threaten someone, how to, 169-170

threatening, when someone is, 83-84

time off, how to ask for, 45-46

tone of voice, 152

topic, how to change the, 33-34

treat others, how to, 151

trust of others, gaining the, 120

trust, engaging, 101

underperforming employee, 65-66

understand, how leaders say they don't, 184

urgency, how to express, 68

violent, when someone is, 99-100

vocabulary, expanding, 20

voice, tone of, 152

walk away, be willing to, 120

work, at, 41-69
    overview of, 41-43

write like a leader, 43

yelling at you, when someone is, 95-96

yes, how leaders say, 181

About the
Author

Patrick Alain is an internationally known video game developer. His titles include the number-one best-sellers "Grand Theft Auto," "Red Dead Redemption," and the "Midnight Club" series. He was born in Paris, France, and has lived in a number of countries throughout his life. Fluent in five languages, Alain attributes much of his success to his ability to function as a vital participant in large, multilingual teams. This book is the product of 10 years of research on leadership. It is Alain's goal to share his knowledge regarding one of the most invaluable skills in life: *taking command of every situation.* Alain lives in San Diego, California, with his wife and daughter. He holds a Master's degree from the University of Paris.